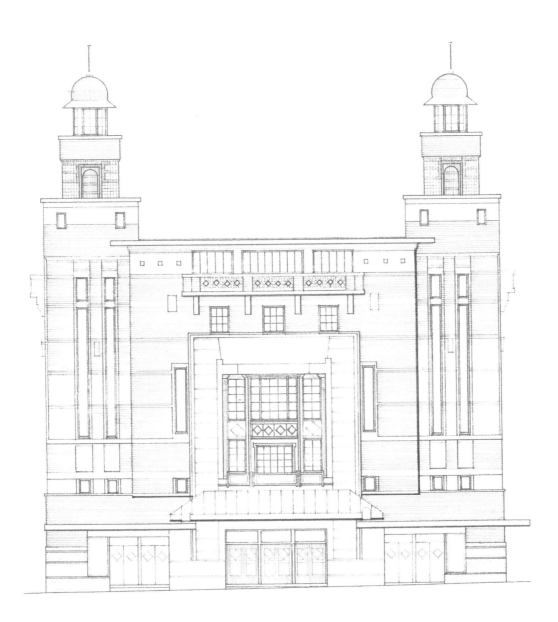

Alhambra

Glasgow

www.glasgowalhambra.co.uk

© Graeme Smith 2011

Published by
Glasgow Publications

Designed by
Cameron Smith

Printed in Scotland by
Bell & Bain Ltd

ISBN 978-0955942013

By the Same Author

The Theatre Royal - Entertaining a Nation

www.glasgowtheatreroyal.co.uk

Alhambra

Glasgow

Graeme Smith

Welcome to the Alhambra

The most advanced theatre in Britain, the Alhambra opened in 1910 and stayed ahead of other theatres. Famous for glamour and humour, variety, ballet, pantomime, musicals, opera, drama and dance the Alhambra expressed the prowess of Glasgow and its environs. Expanding in London, Glasgow and Paris its managing director Sir Alfred Butt gave "the best of European and American Vaudeville attractions" in the "Resort of the Elite."

Alhambra`s eminent architect Sir John Burnet was awarded the Royal Gold Medal of the Royal Institute of British Architects, one of only a few to be recognised in this way, and his firm went on to design the Empire Exhibition, 1938. The Alhambra was one of a handful of super-large theatres in Britain. Its founders supported cinema, jazz, cabaret and ballrooms.

Alhambra pantomimes were the hallmark of quality and spectacle. A showcase for musicals and premieres, it was also the birthplace of Mona Inglesby`s International Ballet company; the heart of Scotland`s largest-ever repertory company, the Wilson Barrett Company; and the venue of Scotland`s first Royal Variety performances, attended by Queen Elizabeth. The theatre`s *Five Past Eight* shows presented by Howard & Wyndham were unequalled in Britain.

In a whole range of restaurants from Miss Rombach`s to the Rogano pre-theatre and post-theatre meals were available, three courses from 2/- (two shillings). After-theatre dancing was promoted by ballrooms for the pleasure of patrons to continue their evening.

For over forty years it was an independently owned theatre - a venture of London and Glasgow, the first step in Sir Alfred Butt emerging as the Napoleon of Variety, and the promoter of scintillating musicals. In 1954 it became the premier theatre of Howard & Wyndham, a company born in the city. Their majestic theatre buildings survive today in Glasgow (2), Edinburgh (2), Newcastle, Manchester, and Liverpool...........all except their flagship....... the Alhambra.

The Alhambra was a modern theatre, its entertainment exuberant.

Contents

Yes, Yes, Yvette

On Monday 19th December 1910 carriages lined up round the new building. Variety now attracted all social classes. Many went in evening dress. The immense Alhambra opened its doors to the surging crowd that besieged it. Soon every nook and cranny was occupied, and hundreds of people were left outside.

After a lively overture from the 30 players of the orchestra, Miss Mary Grey - actress daughter in law of the Lord Mayor of London, no less - stepped in front of the curtains and sang God Save the King. The evening had begun. There were 14 turns, with France's audacious Yvette Guilbert as the main attraction, act number one, singing four songs. The programme declared:

> The Alhambra will be run as a place of family resort, to which a man can take his wife and daughters without fear, and all the highest class of talent obtainable from all parts of the world will be put upon the boards.

Newspapers reported that the managing director **Alfred Butt**:

> ..pays periodical visits to Paris, Berlin, Vienna, Budapest, Madrid, Copenhagen, New York and Chicago keen on the lookout for any turn that may appeal to his British audience.

> Yvette Guilbert is indeed comedy, French comedy personified. Full of grace and charm, she invariably fascinates her audiences alike by her singing and her acting. Her rendering of an old Scottish song "the Auld Man" was rather a bold effort. Of course in her own French songs she was at home, her charming style being much appreciated by those who seemed to understand her, with the gallery expressing its perplexion. The other artistes were all of the highest class, brought from America, Italy, and the best known continental centres of amusement. Some pretty coloured films from the Bioscope completed the performance after which Mr Alfred Butt addressed the audience.

In the house, the soft blue-grey-green of the colour scheme greatly helps the general sense of absolute comfort with the most perfect elegance. The drop curtain and general drapery all in rose velvet, with touches of grey, contrast admirably with the rich crimson of the seats and carpets, whilst the great broad masses of gold about the ceiling and the arch of the

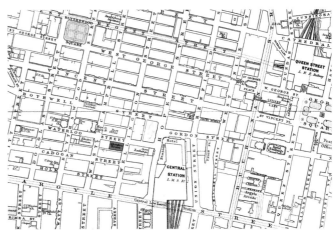

(above)
Alhambra on street map

(opposite)
Alhambra Theatre painting by Robert Eadie RSW

Busy Argyle Street

proscenium achieve a superb value in the completion of the artistic effect.

Construction, starting in May, was taking longer than expected and the target of September was missed. For opening night a slip was placed in the programme saying that

Although every effort has been made, it has been impossible to COMPLETELY finish the Building in time for the Opening. We ask patrons to make due allowance for any temporary imperfections.

One was the ceiling plaster work. The roof was complete but the plasterers had to work night and day to finish it, and buckets full of beer were hoisted up to them at regular intervals.

The following week Edmund Payne and George Grossmith junior, foremost comedians on the British musical comedy stage took pride of place on the vaudeville stage. Josephine la Barte at the piano, playing the latest melodies, was one of many lady pianists onstage in theatres – pit orchestras being all-male. And young Percy Honri, Britain's concertina king, billed himself as "a Concert-in-a turn" in his great musical scene "Concordia."

Still More Theatres

All roads and tramcars led to the Alhambra. Harry Lauder leading the Theatre Royal's pantomime at the top of Hope Street noticed a drop in his audiences as people went off to see the new theatre. More were to open. On the Alhambra opening the weekly Glasgow Programme wrote:

Glasgow during the past few years has been going on increasing the number of places of amusement, until we begin to ask ourselves the question: where will it stop? Every new House eclipses its predecessor in grandeur and style. The Baillie magazine commented:

Alhambra Theatre

Corner of Wellington & Waterloo Street

Managing Director—
Mr. ALFRED BUTT, *of the Palace Theatre, London*

ONE PERFORMANCE NIGHTLY.
MATINEES EVERY WEDNESDAY AT 2

GRAND OPENING NIGHT

MONDAY, 19th DECEMBER
Doors open at 7   Commence 7-30

Special Features
HIGH-CLASS VARITIES
MAGNIFICENT ORCHESTRA
EXCLUSIVE BIOSCOPE PICTURES
(from Palace Theatre, London)
UNPARALLELED PROGRAMME
Important Engagement of
YVETTE GUILBERT
The Famous Parisian Diseuse from the Palace Theatre, London.

ADAMS and WARD Comic Eccentrics	CYRIL CLENSY The Famous Mimic

8—SAXONES—8
From the Broadway Theatre, New York, in their Scenic Novelty, "The Dressing Room."

BRUNO PITROT Novel Act on Mobile Bar	LEONIE DIXON Comedienne & Dancer

THE RITCHIE TROUPE
of Comedy Cyclists
SELECTION BY ORCHESTRA, "Melodious Memories"

THE BIOSCOPE	THE BROKER

BEN ALI
Troupe of Whirling Arabs
THE 3 ATHLETAS
Beautiful French Girls in Feats of Strength
MARY GREY
From Daly's Theatre, London
AND
LES TROMBETTAS
From the Palace Theatre, London, with a Merry Melange.
ALL SEATS EXCEPT AMPHITHEATRE AND GALLERY CAN BE RESERVED
PRICES OF ADMISSION—
Private Boxes, £1 1s. and 10s. 6d.   Orchestra Stalls, 3s.
Dress Circle, 2s. 6d.   Stalls, 2s.   Family Circle, 1s. 6d.
Amphi. (Tip-up Chairs), 9d.   Gallery (Upholstered) 6d.
Seats may be booked at Peterson, Sons & Co., 152 Buchanan Street, 10 a.m. to 4 p.m.   Sats., 10 a.m. to 1 p.m.
NO EARLY DOORS.   NO BOOKING FEES.

Soon one will not see the city for houses of entertainment. And the funny thing about it is that they all attract large audiences. In the circumstances, it might be well if the churches were to adopt some of the variety idea into their services. Perhaps if they sandwiched a music-hall comedian or two or a cinematograph show before and after the sermon they would be assured of huge congregations.

Pantomimes were under way at the Royal, Pavilion, Royalty in Sauchiehall Street, Grand in Cowcaddens, Princess's in Gorbals, and more; the King's had its musicals, the Empire in Sauchiehall Street, Coliseum in Eglinton Street, Metropole in Stockwell Street and others their variety. Violinist Fritz Kreisler was playing at St. Andrews Halls. Carnivals and circuses were full, including Hengler's across the road from the Alhambra, with its great water spectacle, Mexico.

Plans were declared that month for more theatres, the Savoy Theatre opening in a year's time in Hope Street, the Olympia at Bridgeton Cross, and the West End Playhouse/Empress Theatre at St George's Cross soon after that.

Only a very few theatres in Britain were larger than the Alhambra and it would continue as the largest in Alfred Butt's expansion plans. Justifiably it announced itself as **"The Resort of the Elite".**

(above)
Sketches at the Alhambra

GLASGOW
ALHAMBRA

Waterloo and Wellington

The Alhambra's corner site was the most central of all theatres and enjoyed a popular pedigree – Waterloo and Wellington.

Growing westwards from Glasgow Cross many of the city's new streets took the names of successes in the Napoleonic Wars, naval victories in St Vincent, the Nile, Copenhagen – which became Hope Street after Admiral Sir George Johnstone Hope - and battles including Corunna, and finally Waterloo in 1815. Wellington Street opened up from Argyle Street, carrying the Duke's name, and an equestrian statue of him was unveiled in front of the Royal Exchange.

Wellington Church

Before 1827 the site of what would be the Alhambra was a green field. Wellington Street Church opened on it that year at the south west corner of Waterloo Street. It was the largest United Presbyterian church in the city, the congregation's earlier kirk having been in Cheapside Street, Anderston (its first member married there was Henry Bell, inventor of the Comet, the first seagoing steamship in the world.) The new site found "was close to but well west of the city centre, with forbidding approaches across fields, but a good road from Argyle Street." Expanding further, the congregation moved in 1885 to another new site, the current Wellington Church in University Avenue opposite the new buildings of the University.

The Waterloo Rooms

Thomas Jenkins stepped forward as the new owner of the former church which he renamed the Waterloo Rooms, adding it to his city wide chain of dining rooms. Walter Freer, who presided over the Good Templars' Wellington Palace music hall in Gorbals, was appointed manager, overseeing the re-construction of the building to the designs of architect John Burnet, father of architect Sir John Burnet, and developing it as one of the city's social venues before doing the same for Glasgow Corporation's St Andrews Halls, City Halls and others. Journalist Eddie Ashton recalls:

> The Waterloo Rooms, for long a leading centre for that most exclusive of select Glasgow divertissements, the Soiree, Concert, and Ball, to which discreet young ladies took a chaperone and prudent young gentlemen a spare starched collar.

(top) Wellington Street Church

(bottom) Royal Exchange at dawn

(opposite)

Theatre programme cover, Trade adverts.

Glasgow thrived as the Second City of the Empire, trading with every continent. Its companies and their headquarters included shipping, shipbuilding, railways, locomotives, engineering, bridge-building, coal, steel, oil, chemicals, explosives; cotton, textiles, leather, furniture; tobacco, whisky, brewing, food manufacturing; printing and publishing; banks and insurance. Everything from a needle to an anchor! On the Clyde, in 1910, some 250 ships were launched from a score of shipyards.

Catering for People

Thomas Jenkins started as church officer of Hope Street Baptist Church, later of Adelaide Place, and was chosen in 1860 by philanthropist and temperance campaigner **Thomas Corbett**, of a long established Gorbals family, to manage a pioneering project, which 60 years later was still regarded by the US government as a benchmark in improving the food of industrialised workers. Corbett and his wife Janet Gibson of Hillhead despaired of the lack of good, cheap, clean, wholesome food for working class people and the oversupply of public houses selling costly liquor and meals. Nothing was being done about it.

(below) Duke of Wellington, Thomas Jenkins, Dining Room Token

DUKE OF WELLINGTON.

With Jenkins as manager he started the **Great Western Cooking Depot and Dining Rooms**, firstly in the Sailors Home at the Broomielaw. Central kitchens were built in Pitt Street near Argyle Street. Ultimately there were 32 branch Dining Rooms in the city and suburbs, next to offices, factories, cotton mills and the new shipyards. Corbett encouraged employers to change their very early starting times pointing out that fed and healthy workers were better. One branch in High Street was especially for students attending the University. All were fully equipped with stores, ladies dining room, newspapers and periodicals supplied, and non-alcoholic beverages in abundance. Each course was 1d, a three course breakfast was 3d and a five course dinner 5d. Dinners included soup, roast beef, corned beef, mince, steaks, plum or rice pudding. Prime Minister Gladstone and his wife came, declined a top table and sat with the workers, insisting on paying their 5d for dinner.

The annual profits went to good causes including the first money for William Quarrier to start his Orphan Homes; Seaside Convalescent Homes down the Clyde; and the YMCA. Corbett started the first Working Men's Club in Scotland (in the Trongate) which then promoted, with his help, the Glasgow Industrial Exhibition of 1865, its profits being used for educational purposes. He also built bowling-greens in Glasgow to provide alternatives to going to public houses, and dwelling houses for working families in Glasgow and many more in London.

In 1870 Corbett sold the Great Western Cooking Depot and early Dining Rooms to Thomas Jenkins, with profits continuing to go to charity. The purveyor expanded as a wholesale and retail butcher and partner of a dairy business. The Baillie magazine commented "Special care is paid to the cooking, and the waiters are trim, handy girls, who move about with an abundance of quietness and celerity."

In full swing from 1885 the **Waterloo Rooms** could hold 1200 people in the new main Pillar Hall. There were Lesser Halls, refreshment rooms, and cooking kitchens above the crypt, whose burial remains were re-interred elsewhere. Dinners, weddings, balls and soirees, recitals and concerts

multiplied, especially of Highland associations, Clan and County associations, Gaelic societies and choirs. Music-hall nights included productions of *Rob Roy*, the favourite comedian Willie Frame, and the debut of tenor JW Bowie. The largest of choirs was the Social Reform community choir of 800 members!

It was the first venue in Glasgow to hear the phonograph, and later the first to see moving pictures, re-called as "badly focussed, jerky, spasmodic representations of prize fights." Industries conferred and ex-hibited, meetings convened on trade, politics, social reform, trade union-ism, and sport.

(below) The Glasgow Industrial Exhibition 1865, Scottish Labour Party membership, Keir Hardie

Birthplace of the Labour Party

The most important national event was in August 1888 when the first Labour Party in Britain was formed. After a march and rally, the meeting in the Waterloo Rooms voted Keir Hardie MP as chairman of the Scottish Labour Party, RB Cunninghame Graham MP as

secretary, and Neil Mactaggart, treasurer, whose son (Sir) John Mactaggart became the noted house builder.

Corbett's son Cameron Corbett (the first Lord Rowallan) continued the family philanthropy, gifting to the citizens of Glasgow the estate of Rouken Glen, and the huge highland estate of Ardgoil between Loch Long and Loch Goil.

Culture on the Clyde

New art galleries and a museum opened at Kelvingrove and a new art school

now sat on the crest of Garnethill, designed by a new architect Charles Rennie Mackintosh. To the city's theatres, halls, circuses and skating rinks were added new-fangled picture houses, including twelve in Sauchiehall Street alone. In the confident Edwardian era six grand theatres opened making a total of around 20 theatres and music halls. All followed the footsteps of Christina and James Baylis who, in the 1860s, created the large Scotia Music Hall in Stockwell Street and the Theatre Royal in Hope Street.

(above)
James Baylis
(right) Miss Rombach advert, Hengler's Cirque, Wellington Street, Grosvenor Restaurant.

Directly across Waterloo Street sat Albert Hengler's Grand Cirque in an immense building designed by theatre architect Frank Matcham, attracting thousands each week to its circus entertainments, water spectaculars, musical equestrian extravaganzas, vaudeville, skating shows and pantomime. One of Neil Munro's delightful stories of Para Handy and his Clyde puffer crew tells of a night out in Wellington Street at Waterloo Street, with Hurricane Jack being very busy on a double date, one lady being with him at a soiree in the

Waterloo Rooms and another with him at Hengler's!

More and more dinners, balls, concerts and meetings were held in the large new hotels and in the Waterloo Rooms, and the magnificent Grosvenor Restaurant, with its marble staircase, opened in Gordon Street in 1899. Tea-rooms and restaurants multiplied including Cranston's, James Craig's, Cooper's, Miss Rombach's, Miss Buick's and, later, Wendy's. To favourites such as Sloan's, His Lordship's Larder, F& F's, Danny Brown's, the Royal, at the foot of West Nile Street, and other oyster bars and chop houses, were added more licensed restaurants in the new century including the Grant Arms in Argyle Street, and Rogano in Royal Exchange, later joined in Hope Street by One-O-One, and Guy's further up the street. Those with very large wallets would be attracted to the sparkling Malmaison in the Central Hotel.

After Thomas Jenkins died the Waterloo Rooms were put up for sale and the site in such a busy location attracted the attention of four promoters, two from Glasgow and two from London.

(above) Waterloo Rooms Demolition drawn by JH Mackenzie RSW

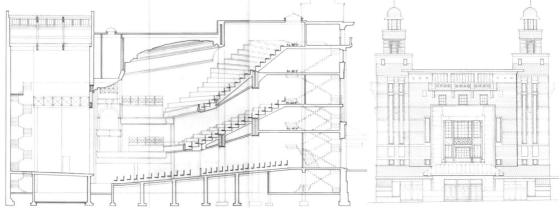

Glasgow Alhambra Ltd

Soon the Waterloo Rooms were cleared and a very new style emerged. Clean cut. Ahead of itself. Who were the owners and who was the architect?

Architectural historians, Andor Gomme and David Walker say of its architect **Sir John James Burnet**:

> He was the best known architect of his time, with a reputation that dwarfed Charles Rennie Mackintosh. His contribution to the city centre is the greatest by a single architect with the possible exception of Greek Thomson.

Alfred Butt, age 31, had far horizons. He was improving the tone of music-hall, enhancing the quality of acts, putting *variety* into Variety, and setting prices attractive to all classes. He was now challenging the size and power of Sir Edward Moss, from Greenock, who headed the largest grouping of variety theatres in the world. During 1909 Alfred Butt formed a trans-Atlantic syndicate which announced plans for new theatres starting with the Alhambra Glasgow, to be followed by the Orpheum Berlin, the Victoria Palace London, the Palace Paris, and the Palace New York. Each would have its own investors.

Butt and his London Palace Theatre chairman **Ernest Polden**, whose printing company had as its largest client the British Army, met with two Glasgow businessmen **John P Kinghorn**, iron broker and merchant, and **John Rowan**, stock broker. The lawyers for the new company were Beyfus and Beyfus. In November 1909 the Prospectus was issued inviting the public to buy shares in the **Glasgow Alhambra Ltd,** with Polden as chairman and Butt as managing director.

Eight hundred people invested, from housewife and widow to engineers and captains, patternmakers to plumbers, dressmaker to hospital matron, farrier to messenger, foundry manager and salesmen.

(opposite)

Alhambra side view.

Architectural section drawing 1910.

Alhambra frontage, drawn from plans, by John Hepburn FRIAS.

(below)

Auditorium from stage.

The founder directors (the promoters) were not the largest shareholders - the top four were a solicitor, stockbroker, John Fisher, warehouse merchant, and James Ferguson, shipbuilder at Port Glasgow. The company would remain an independent company in the Alfred Butt fold.

Prospectus

This Company has been formed to acquire the valuable site at the south-west corner of the junction of Waterloo Street and Wellington Street, Glasgow at present occupied by the Waterloo Rooms; to erect a handsome and commodious building embodying the latest principles and ideas in theatre construction, and to carry on the same as a first-class Variety Theatre.

The site is admirably adapted for the purpose, placed as it is in close proximity to the large Railway Termini, and in the immediate vicinity of the principal car routes of the city. It is distant from the Central Station about 100 yards and within a few minutes walk of St Enoch and Queen Street Stations. The car routes in Argyle Street, Hope Street and Bothwell Street may be said to encircle the building on three sides. While those in Renfield Street are within a short distance.

The site is practically an island one, permitting the Theatre to be filled and emptied in the shortest possible time, and has the further advantage of being very free from noise.

(below)

London Palace Theatre.

Hippodrome, New York

Pioneering construction

Nearby, Burnet was completing a number of office blocks and extending the opulent pile of the Clyde Navigation Trust of which John Kinghorn was a member. To Burnet's design the Alhambra rose in its steel frame, clad in brick, guided by engineer George Leslie Allen and his Allen Construction Company of West Regent Street. The following year Burnet again chose the Allen Construction Company to build the (equally) pioneering steel-framed Kodak Building in London's Kingsway.

The American Influence

JJ Burnet enthused about American invention and styling, translating much of it into his buildings in Britain. He knew Alfred Butt shared the vitality and showmanship of America. Burnet would be fully aware of New York's newest, largest and most vibrant theatre, the red brick Hippodrome, which opened in 1905. Designed by JH Morgan and modified by Dundee-born Thomas W Lamb (one of over 300 theatres and cinemas he was responsible for in the USA and elsewhere), the Hippodrome was described as "Beaux-Arts with a Moorish Revival twist". It advertised itself as the "Largest Playhouse in the World" seating 5300 people, and had state of the art technology.

By a happy coincidence the Hippodrome's director and producer of mammoth musical spectaculars was RH Burnside, from Glasgow, the son of a manager of the Gaiety/Empire Theatre in Sauchiehall Street and of actress Margaret Thorne, leading lady in James Baylis's pantomimes of the 1860s at

Alfred Butt

Alfred Butt was a surprise to all. A young lawyer, Alfred Beyfus, of the Beyfus household in one of London's elegant squares, had an affair with the upstairs maid with the result that young Alfred Butt came into the world in 1878.

Earlier in the 19th century the Beyfus family migrated from Hamburg to Glasgow and London, becoming general traders – including yarns, leeches and steel pens – and developing as furniture dealers, money lenders, diamond merchants and solicitors. In London the firm of Beyfus & Beyfus gained a reputation as pugnacious lawyers. Many clients were from the theatre world, including Richard D'Oyly Carte, opera singer Caruso, and dancer Diaghilev.

Mr D'Oyly Carte's newly built Royal English Opera House in London failed and the building in Shaftesbury Avenue emerged as the Palace Variety Theatre, largely controlled by the Beyfus family. After training as an accountant at Harrods, where a director was married to one of Alfred Beyfus's sisters, the young Alfred Butt joined the Palace, learning to manage and produce variety shows, which became spectacular revues, and becoming managing director in 1906. His aunt Gertrude Beyfus was married to Michael Garcia, partner in Simons, Jacobs & Co, fruit importers, headquartered in Glasgow and chaired by Michael Simons, who in 1895 created Howard & Wyndham Ltd, which became the largest company in Britain of drama theatres.

(above)
Alfred Butt

A Vanity Fair magazine feature about him in 1911 shows Maud Allen, one of his principal artistes, some thought his mistress, in her controversial *Salome* dance. He introduced opera singers and dramatists, paying more than they got in drama theatres and was first in introducing classical ballet to Britain. He believed "good art was good business" – providing it at popular prices - and vied with impresario Oswald Stoll in importing Russian talent.

He let it be known he wanted to become Chancellor of the Exchequer and in a few years time he added a career in politics. He was successful at the casino tables of France, and the racecourses on both sides of the Channel.

the new Theatre Royal. In 1915 Burnside was asked by Alfred Butt to take control of the stage direction of all his theatres in Britain, at $20,000 a year.

Moorish Red Walls

Using the colour and cube shape of the Alhambra in Granada, the new theatre was finished in red brick, banded with black, and panels of white-glazed tile towards the top. There was also white tiling at ground level under the pavement canopies. Twin towers added above the cube were *chatris*,

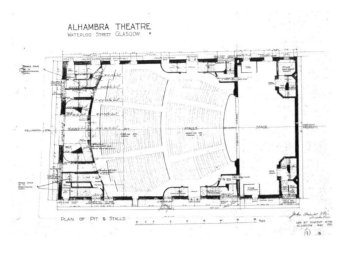

ALHAMBRA THEATRE
WATERLOO STREET GLASGOW

PLAN OF PIT & STALLS

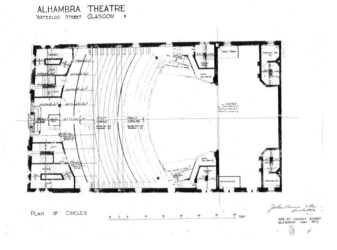

ALHAMBRA THEATRE
WATERLOO STREET GLASGOW

PLAN OF CIRCLES

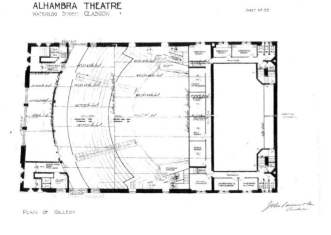

ALHAMBRA THEATRE
WATERLOO STREET GLASGOW

PLAN OF GALLERY

reflecting the importance of trade to India, jewel in the crown of the British Empire. A *chatri* in India, usually with four columns, allowed cool air to those sitting under it, and chatri domes were added to temples and other important buildings. The cool air entering the theatre was thought by customers to be too cool, and adjustments were made.

Burnet's new project reflected some of his Athenaeum theatre styling in Buchanan Street and some of the Hippodrome's exterior and interior. He rejected the rococo wedding cake style used in so many theatres. The Alhambra interior and balconies were in a restrained Louis XVI style, and the colour schemes were by the top interior decorators Guthrie & Wells. Above the boxes on one side of the auditorium was the Scottish lion rampant, and on the other the English lions couchant, with Glasgow's coat of arms on the centre of the proscenium arch. The theatre and land cost £60,000.

The frontage on Wellington Street was 83 feet wide and the theatre 140 feet long, before a major extension in the 1920s, and the stage opening was 37 feet. In the 1960s the stage was widened to 75 feet for the *Five Past Eight* shows.

Designed for 3000, it was decided to cut the numbers standing and it opened for 2,436, a number that would remain constant; the Stalls and Pit seating 952, the Circle 628, and the Amphitheatre and Gallery holding over 800 including 100 standing. There were Boxes on each side of the Stalls and Circle.

Entering through the six swing doors of mahogany, the small elliptical vestibule flanked with two pay boxes was floored in white marble with marble pillars and stairs leading down to the stalls and up to the circle. The vestibule ceiling was picked out in gold. Stained glass windows adorned the stairways. Entrances nearer the corners led up to the gods, past a pay box. All the seats were tip-up armchairs including in the amphitheatre. The gallery benches were upholstered in leather at a time when theatres were still using wooden benches. Unusually each of the huge curving rows of this tier dipped towards the centre aisle, giving perfect sightlines.

The bar saloon for Front Stall patrons backed onto the bar saloon for Pit patrons, but entered separately. The Front Stalls also had two small lounges on either side of the auditorium. Up in the Circle the bar saloon facing Waterloo Street had next to it a Bioscope enclosure for the short films shown at the end of each bill.

There were 15 dressing rooms at first, the stage door opening to Waterloo Street, with the stage manager's room to one side of the stage. The scenery door was round in Wellington Lane, with a hand props store adjacent. Under the stage was the musical director's room, band room and carpenter's area. In the space directly above the very deep proscenium arch, and served by a corridor round three sides of the tall fly-tower, were the offices for "enquiries and typist", company secretary and treasurer, check room, bill room, janitor room, and female attendants.

The theatre's seats were a new design, inlaid with Sheraton mahogany. These were made in England, causing shareholders to ask why there were not made by the many high-class furniture makers in Glasgow and Beith. The day before the opening there was a private view for guests including the Lord Provost McInnes Shaw, afternoon tea being served.

Kinemacolor – "Eighth Wonder of the World"

Alfred Butt was also interested in cinema. In 1909 after meeting film producer Charles Urban he became the majority shareholder in Britain's new National Colour Kinematographe Company to exploit its wonders and technologies, in particular the invention in 1906 of natural colour motion photography by George A Smith. The first presentation of colour films to a paying audience in the world took place at Butt's Palace Theatre in London on 26th

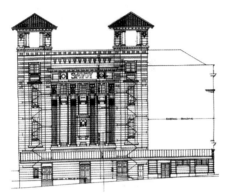

February 1909, with a programme of 21 Kinemacolor short films. Each day's variety bill now included Kinemacolor film.

Butt arranged national distribution by creating the Provincial Palace Ltd linking firms across the country including one started by John Kinghorn in Glasgow. Highly successful as it was the Kinematographe Company folded in 1914 after protracted lawsuits from others challenging the pioneering patent.

London

In 1911 he also began operating London's Gaiety Theatre, owned by Solomon Joel, millionaire trader in South African diamonds and gold. That same year Butt started the building of another new theatre, the Victoria Palace, with 65% of the money coming from an American in New York, a person not connected to the stage - but whose wife was an aspiring comedy actress. This was Frank Gould, railroad heir and Francophile who owned a string of casinos on the Riviera. It opened in 1912 topped with a statue of one of Butt's discoveries, the ballerina Anna Pavlova.

In 1914, this time with backing by Solly Joel, Butt bought the Queen's and Globe Theatres, followed next year by the Adelphi. Joel's wayward daughter Doris Joel was a composer and lyricist for revues, and taught a young Noel Coward how to write music for the stage.

Paris and Berlin

As part of the new syndicate involving Morris Meyerfeld, of America's Orpheum circuit, who was known as the "Rockefeller of Vaudeville," a site was leased to Butt and Meyerfeld in 1913 in Paris, near the Grand Opera, to build the first of a series of theatres on the Continent. Construction was delayed until the end of the Great War. One did open under the Orpheum flag in Berlin in 1914 seating 2000, opening with the French singer and dancer

Sir John J Burnet and his Team

Sir John James Burnet was eminent in architecture and had studied at the Ecole des Beaux-Arts in Paris. He became a member of the American Institute of Architects, President of the Glasgow Institute of Architects and a Governor of the Glasgow School of Art. His surviving work in Glasgow includes the Clyde Navigation Trust (Clydeport) in Robertson Street, Barony Church, Charing Cross Mansions, the poignant Cenotaph in George Square, Glasgow University Students Union, Glasgow University Chapel and the American styled offices of Atlantic Chambers, Waterloo Chambers and North British Insurance, 200 St Vincent Street. In London his clients included General Accident, Selfridges, Kodak and the British Museum.

This was his second theatre, the first being the exquisite but small red-sandstoned Athenaeum still existing in Buchanan Street. For the Alhambra project the chief draughtsman in Glasgow was the legendary William John Blain, Burnet's right-hand man, and a President of the Glasgow Architectural Association. After the Alhambra was completed Blain left the firm, feeling he should have been made a partner, and started a new partnership which concentrated on cinemas and theatres.

In the same Modern Movement manner as the Alhambra, Burnet designed, just two years later, the advanced Wallace Scott Tailoring Institute (complete with its own concert hall and leisure gardens), owned by RW Forsyth Ltd, where Dexter clothing and waterproofs were made and exported worldwide. It continues in Cathcart as one of Scottish Power's headquarter buildings. For his lifetime service to architecture he was awarded the Royal Gold Medal by the Royal Institute of British Architects. His continuing firm of Burnet, Tait & Lorne designed the Empire Exhibition 1938, in Bellahouston Park, attended by 13 million visitors.

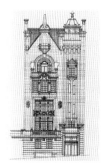

(left)
Sir John James Burnet

(above)
Athenaeum Theatre
Kodak House
(opposite)
Wallace Scott Tailoring Institute

Savoy Theatre, Hope Street, designed by James Miller

Mlle Polaire, renowned for her 13 inch waist. Plans were laid for Hamburg, Frankfurt and Cologne. Austria and Russia were also being thought about.

International Syndicate

Every year from 1907 Morris Meyerfeld, international banker and owner of the Orpheum circuit of theatres from San Francisco to Chicago, toured Europe looking to link with businesses – all the more important in the aftermath of the San Francisco earthquake. Butt saw the advantages. In a concerted move with Meyerfeld he bid successfully in 1910 to take over the large group of theatres in Britain, and one each in Paris and Brussels, which had been developed by the late Tom Barrasford, whose creations included Glasgow's

MOSS-THORNTON-STOLL
CIRCUIT.

Chairman : Sir H. E. MOSS.   Managing Director : OSWALD STOLL.
Assisting Director and Chief of Staff : FRANK ALLEN.

THIRTY-SEVEN VARIETY THEATRES.
Over £2,086,000 Capital.
CONSTITUTING THE
GREATEST AGGREGATION OF
VARIETY THEATRES IN THE WORLD.

LONDON HIPPODROME

The Empire, Glasgow · The Empire, Dublin
The Empire, Edinburgh · The Empire, Belfast
The Empire, Newcastle · The Empire, Coventry
The Empire, Leeds · The Empire, Sunderland
The Empire, Bradford · The Palace, Hull
The Empire, Sheffield · The Palace, Leicester
The Empire, Birmingham · The Palace, Bordesley
The Empire, Liverpool · The Granville, Walham Green
The Empire, Cardiff · The Manchester Hippodrome
The Empire, Swansea · The Glasgow Coliseum
The Empire, Newport · Olympia, Liverpool
The Empire, Nottingham · His Majesty's Theatre of Varieties,
The Empire, Ardwick, Manchester · Walsall
The Empire, South Shields · The Reading Theatre
The Empire, Hackney, London, N.E. · The Richmond Theatre, Richmond
The Empire, Holloway, London, N. · The Philharmonic Hall, Cardiff
The Empire, New Cross, London, S.E. · The Zoo and Hippodrome, Glasgow
The Empire, Stratford, London, E.
The Empire, Shepherd's Bush,
London, W.

CO-OPERATIVE OFFICES :
CRANBOURN MANSIONS, CRANBOURN ST., W.C.
Where all communications should be addressed.

Artistes are requested to note our calls every week in the leading variety papers.

(left) Anna Pavlova, Mlle Polaire, Martin Beck, Sir Edward Moss

(right) Kinemacolor advert, Moss advert

Pavilion Theatre. Weeks later a group of theatres led by Walter de Frece, husband of Vesta Tilley, joined the new combine, the **Variety Theatres Controlling Company Ltd**, under its first chairman Alfred Butt.

At the same time Butt and the Orpheum's general manager Martin Beck announced the international syndicate, called the **Beck-Butt Circuit**, joined also by the major theatre combines around New York. The Los Angeles Times' headline ran "World Variety Circuit Formed." Performers could now have three years' consecutive booking in the States and Europe without retracing their route. Alfred Butt, for the new British combine, represented the syndicate in Europe, and created links with South Africa and Australia.

Butt and Beck shared similar outlooks, with Beck "booking opera singers, classical musicians, and ballet dancers, even if he was the only one in the audience who understood them." Beck's objective was "To make the Orpheum circuit bring the highest forms of art within the reach of the people with the slimmest purses." In 1913 Martin Beck opened the Palace Theatre in New York which became the top vaudeville house in America for twenty years.

The Napoleon of Vaudeville

On both sides of the Atlantic, Alfred Butt was known as "The Boy Manager", on account of his youthful looks. Many an artiste would pass him in the hallway and ask if the manager was in. Once his international plans rolled out, the Washington Times called him "The Napoleon of Vaudeville." Butt's theatre power now matched that of Sir Edward Moss and his associate Oswald Stoll.

John P Kinghorn

John Pitilla Kinghorn traded in the Royal Exchange as an iron-broker, as did the Colville brothers before setting up their steel works in Motherwell, and Andrew Bonar Law before becoming Prime Minister. He worked in the Glasgow Ironworks at Dixon's Blazes, Govanhill before becoming an iron-ore importer and coal exporter. He was an elected member of the Clyde Navigation Trust, and a stalwart of the Glasgow Art Club, amassing a large collection of paintings. Kinghorn was a director of Glasgow Alhambra until his passing in 1929.

He was also director of an "Electric Theatres" company which opened the first purpose-built cinema in Glasgow, albeit behind the facade of an existing warehouse in Sauchiehall Street. This was the Charing Cross Electric Theatre, designed by George Boswell, which opened on 12th May 1910 showing films in Kinemacolor, the first time in Scotland, to the amazement of the daily crowds and financial health of the promoters. The Glasgow Herald reported:

"White and black film has become established and also brush-coloured film but natural colour motion photography was still to be attained – this problem has now been solved by what is known as the Urban-Smith process, devised by George A Smith of Brighton, the father of the British film industry. The new process is described as "kinemacolour". A local company The West of Scotland Electric Theatres Ltd has acquired the sole rights of Kinemacolour in Glasgow and the West of Scotland. All the new pictures were remarkably true to life without the aid of artificial retouching."

The cinema was later remodelled as the Locarno Ballroom, complete with club-rooms and garaging for members, led by the restaurateur and tea-room king James Craig, and former Lord Provost Sir Archibald McInnes Shaw, whose son would become a chairman of the Alhambra.

(above)

The Royal Exchange. Charing Cross Electric Theatre.

(below)

John Rowan

John Rowan

John Rowan guided the birth of the Alhambra. The Baillie wrote in 1914 "the Alhambra is now wonderfully prosperous." His father was the cashier and office manager of Lord Overtoun's chemical works at Shawfield, and put his son in to train with a firm of chartered accountants and stockbrokers. On leaving, John Rowan started his own firm of stockbrokers and is credited with having the first internal private telephone network for business purposes, linking his firm and correspondents in London. He was a writer of verse and published "Spunyarnes in Rhyme" about voyages at sea. In 1930 he became the theatre's chairman, retiring in 1935.

THE WHIP

MR GEORGE DANCES CO

THE ALHAMBRA
6·45 TWICE NIGHTLY 9

Managing Director
Mr ALFRED BUTT

General Manager
Mr JOSEPH WILSON

A MAGNIFICENT and PERFECTLY EQUIPPED VARIETY THEATRE

PROGRAMME

Presenting at all times the BEST of EUROPEAN and AMERICAN VAUDEVILLE ATTRACTIONS

Week commencing MONDAY, 29th APRIL, 1918.

6·15. Two Performances Nightly. 8·20.

MATINEE—WEDNESDAY at 2·30.

WELCOME RETURN OWING TO SENSATIONAL SUCCESS.

ERNEST C. ROLLS
Presents the Great London Success,

TOPSY TURVY

THE GREATEST CAST EVER TOURED, includes the Queen of Revue

JENNIE BENSON

IDA ERNEST   LILIAN TREVOR

TOM DREW

WALTER RIGNOLD   NAN FOSTER

G. S. MELVIN

G. RITCHIE   ERNEST GRATA

FRED A. LESLIE   HYLDA LEWIS

And FULL COMPANY   The whole Produced by ERNEST C. ROLLS

NEXT
WEEK   Miss ELLEN TERRY

THE ALHAMBRA GRAND ORCHESTRA under the direction of EDWARD GROFF.

PRICES AS USUAL

The World is Happily Mad

After a long closure for the hot summer of 1911 when Kelvingrove hosted its third international exhibition – the Scottish Exhibition, attracting 9 million visitors - the Alhambra started two houses a night, which the public expected.

Alfred Butt added variety to Variety. After the overture the first act was frequently a play, musical revue, ballet, or short opera, followed by variety with 6-10 turns, and ending with film. Through the Syndicate, entertainers came from all continents - comics, mimists, singers, illusionists, gymnasts, tumblers, instrumentalists, dancers, whistlers, Arabian whirlers, conjurers, memory men, trick cyclists, quartettes, jugglers, and ventriloquists.

The Bioscope, originally from the London Palace theatre, was now supplied by the Bendon Trading Company, owned by "Prince" William Bendon, the noted ventriloquist-turned-film trader, who created Scotland's first film studio in 1910 at Rouken Glen, where the following year Glasgow Corporation proposed developing Zoological Gardens.

Dance and Ballet

Maud Allan was the most celebrated free-movement dancer, originally a trained pianist in America, moving to dance in San Francisco. After seeing her in Berlin Butt promoted her by skilled publicity and long term appearances in his Palace Theatre attended by royalty. She scandalised because of her sensual dancing and clothing, and because of her bare legs – when tights were thought to be essential.

The Alhambra orchestra was augmented for all her visits in the next 10 years, and variety turns followed. Special matinees were held, with no smoking and no variety. Ladies came to see what dancing without corsets was like. And gentlemen too. In April 1911, making a return visit to Glasgow but her first to the Alhambra, she danced barefoot, as usual, to Greig's *Peer Gynt Suite*, with an encore of Rubinstein's *Valse Caprice*. It was said of her "she is music made visible." She then went on world tours, always appearing with an orchestra of 60. Prime Minister Asquith's wife Margo Tennant paid the rent of her villa in London's Regent's Park, causing more scandal.

The Danish classical ballerina Adeline Genee settled in Britain, later founding the Royal Academy of Dance. From 1911 she appeared in the Alhambra always as the top line in variety, dancing A Dream of Butterflies and Roses, by Gounod, and some of her own compositions including La Camargo. The Imperial Russian Ballet first came in 1912. Popular in Glasgow, Anna Pavlova had fallen out with Alfred Butt, preferring Moss Empires, but came to the Alhambra in the 1920s.

Opera

The first opera in 1911, followed by variety, was Evelyn Millard in a version of *Madame Butterfly*. March saw the first appearance outside London of The Thomas Beecham Grand Opera Company, then only a year old, with a chorus of 60 including soprano Edith Evans, before she turned to acting, with the Glasgow Herald exclaiming:

> A week of extracts from Carmen and Tannhauser. Wagner in a music-hall. Tannhauser a "turn." The old order changeth.

They came back the next year with Carmen, Faust, Il Trovatore and Bohemian Girl. Sir Joseph Beecham took the credit for arranging curtailed versions of opera, and his son conducted. After the interval other variety acts took stage.

Plays

Often at the top of the bill, plays and sometimes scenes from Shakespeare took about one hour – all to catch attention and dramatic effect – followed of course by variety. For one-act plays Butt engaged new playwrights such as GB Shaw, John Galsworthy, JM Barrie, and later James Bridie. H B Irving and Martin Harvey brought their acting companies on occasion. Seymour Hicks put on his own plays, while Sir Herbert Tree put on a play about Rudyard Kipling. Scots born actor and producer William Mollison starred in Richelieu; and the everlasting Mrs Patrick Campbell came with a potted play, and later gave Repertory weeks.

(left) Adeline Genee, Evelyn Millard, Thomas Beecham, Edith Evans, William Mollison

(below) Advert 1911

Before Christmas 1912 the Scottish Repertory Theatre Company, started by Alfred Wareing, gave three new one act plays in a three week season, one of which was by the Belgian playwright Maeterlinck who had won the Nobel Prize. The Company were displaced at the Royalty due to a Kinemacolor film season, and planned to resume full length plays next year under Lewis Casson. But next year they were back, with a London newspaper catching up "I see that the Scottish Repertory has been appearing at the Alhambra. This is the first time a repertory company has appeared at a music-hall." Over the years The Abbey Theatre Irish Players gave weeks of repertory, as did Graham Moffat's company of

ALHAMBRA THEATRE.
Doors Open at 7.   Commence, 7.30.
THE THOMAS BEECHAM GRAND OPERA CO.
WITH FULL CHORUS OF 60 PICKED VOICES.
Positively the First Appearance out of London.
THE FIVE TORNADOS.   RITA & FOSTER.
LILIAN LEA.   CAMPBELL & BRADY.
JOE ARCHER.   HYDE & CODY TRIO.
THE BIOSCOPE WITH EXCLUSIVE PICTURES.
Also JACK ARK.
THE MARIMBA BAND,
Four Marimbreros from Guatemala.
SPECIAL MATINEES at 2 p.m.
FULL PROGRAMME.
Book at Messrs. Paterson, Sons & Co., also at Theatre.

Scottish Players.

Entertaining Variety

In comic singing and dancing extravaganza the John Tiller dancers changed their troupe names and formations as required, the first in the Alhambra being Tiller's Eight Sunshine Girls. Some of his productions had four scenes, with a cast of 100. He had Tiller Schools of Dancing in Berlin, Copenhagen, London, Glasgow, Leeds and other cities, and later in New York.

(above) The Tiller Girls

(right) JM Barrie, John Tiller, JM Hamilton, Nellie Donegan, Alfred Wareing

A favourite was Betty Barclay and a Baritone – presumably most money going to pianist Betty. Josephine La Barte in Songs at the Piano was another, as was the tenor JM Hamilton. Other turns included Reynolds & Donegan, the American Roller Skaters; Donald & Carson, America's favourite Scottish Comedians; Jessie Berg, the Russian Girl with the Fiddle; La Tosca Trio, with opera extracts; Miss Minnie Fenton, the Scotch Girl at the Piano; Herbert Lloyd the King of Diamonds, a comic-juggler from the USA who shed shirt-front after shirt-front during his act, all bejewelled; Trovati, "the Sousa of the Violin"; The Musical McGregors and their xylophones; and The Bleriots, aerial football cyclists. Duncan's Scotch Collies, a fun act continued for about 40 years – with different dogs!

Novel tableaux still had charms, Canova's Living Porcelains plying themselves into huge Dresden figurines and settings. The blind pianist Mendel played tunes requested by the audience. Down the list but high in appeal was Miss Millie Gordon – "She dances with snakes entwined about her neck and body, but she needs no such aid to make her turn interesting."

Karno, Houdini and the Keatons

Fred Karno & His Barmy Army became regulars, his name standing for the comedy of good intentions bungled. He opened at the Alhambra in 1911, in a comedy sketch of Moses and Son, with Stan Jefferson (Stan Laurel) making his professional debut. He had companies of comedians touring Britain and America, including young Charlie Chaplin and Jefferson. Karno became a great exhibitionist, noting in Glasgow the publicity ideas of theatre manager Arthur Jefferson, father of Stan Laurel, who would send round Glasgow a portable zoo cage with a live lion inside mauling a man's body - of course, the body was a dummy. Stan Laurel said: "Fred Karno didn't teach Charlie and me all we know about comedy, he just taught us most of it".

From America came escapologist Harry Houdini, at the same time as

The Keatons, including their 15 year-old son Buster Keaton who went on to make madcap films in Hollywood. Singer Eugene Stratton, creator of the popular song Lily of Laguna, decided to stay in Britain. Other weekly headliners ranged from Julian Rose, the Hebrew comedian, in versions of *Levinsky at the Wedding*, to the Mirza Golem Troupe from Persia presenting "The Slave Dealers" complete with music, camels and acrobats.

Disappearing Tigers

Illusionist Horace Goldin from America had a fast paced show and his signature illusion was Sawing the Lady in Half, but his first week at Waterloo Street had his sensational drama of The Tiger God – when he made a live Bengal tiger disappear. There was a new one next day. Carl Hertz made birdcages and canaries disappear, discovering the canary in the pocket of an audience member. David Devant was the king, appearing in Glasgow for the first time in 1912 and ready with his Indian Rope Trick which he followed with Vice Versa when he turned a man into a woman. In the evenings he led a bill of 11 acts including baritone Peter Melvin, and Moran & Wiser – sensational hat throwers. On his visits Devant presented the magic of levitation, and his Egg Trick involved a member of the audience picking up eggs endlessly produced from a hen on stage. For fans and families there was a Saturday Special Matinee, a 2-hour programme of Devant's Mysteries only. NO VARIETY ARTISTES WILL APPEAR – NO SMOKING WILL BE ALLOWED.

(left) The Keatons, Julian Rose, Horace Goldin, David Devant, Fred Karno Army

Linga Singh –"The Hindu illusionist of high caste" – topped a week at home under the chatri domes of the theatre. One paper reported "He produces six poisonous snakes from nowhere…...... and from the mere half shell of a coconut he produces a fountain of gushing crystal water which flows so long as to fill three large vases. From the third emerges a beautiful girl, dry and untouched by the water." No one could work that out, but some may have tried it themselves!

Pantomime or no Pantomime

In winter, halls staged pantomime or variety. The Alhambra introduced *Follies*, the first of many, and added a week each year of a Touring Pantomime, often from Harry Burns' company. The first in January 1912 was *Dick Whittington & His Cat*, in 11 scenes (and no variety afterwards) with Helen Charles and Peter Bermingham, who was a new comic, remembered for his rich Glasgow accent and for yelling to his off-stage stooge "I've nae chinge, keep the hoarse."

The Vaudeville Follies were "revues", an entertainment

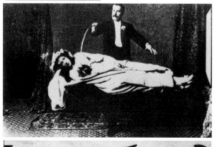

started in Paris in the 1890s. HG Pelissier created this show and gave his wife Fay Compton her start in her stage career. Larger than life, he was a satirist and burlesqued grand opera, musical comedy, and mime. Others would bring more revues, notably Andre Charlot, followed by Albert de Courville who was secretary to Sir Edward Moss and would start London's first jazz club in 1922, Alfred Butt and CB Cochran.

In early 1912, and with no following variety, Kismet, hot off the music-stand, was staged over two weeks in the vivid colours of the Orient. As with Maud Allan, Kismet was "Smoking Prohibited" In the following month the drama unfolded of The Whip in 3 acts and 13 scenes, complete with twelve horses and a travelator for the finale race. The next winter saw a touring pantomime Robinson Crusoe for a week, and a later week of The Forty Thieves.

Britain's First Royal Command Variety Show

The Alhambra took some reflected glory from Alfred Butt's staging of the first public Royal Command Performance in a music-hall attended

(clockwise from top)

Carl Hertz, David Devant advert, Linga Singh, Kismet advert, Kismet bath scene, Pelissier's Follies

by a monarch, King George V and Queen Mary. In 1911 theatres indulged in a frenzy of celebration ahead of the Coronation. There were special performances for play, opera and ballet. Little wonder that variety wanted in. After all the music hall barons had been strenuous in their efforts to achieve respectability, with their eyes on knighthoods.

Sir Edward Moss got Royal agreement for a Command performance in aid of artistes' benevolent funds. He would stage it at his own expense at the Albert Hall, or in Edinburgh as part of the Coronation visit in July. The King agreed to Edinburgh, in the Empire theatre. Unfortunately fire consumed the theatre in May. By this time Sir Edward had become terminally ill. Theatre owners in London vied to hold it the following year, with Alfred Butt being selected by Buckingham Palace and the show was produced by him in his London Palace variety theatre in 1912.

Ragtime, Rimsky and Revues

Australians came to Waterloo Street as did Dutch actors and comics, French mimists, and from Hungary the pianist Vilmos Westonz, who played Wagner and added comedy. Specialty acts like Lipinsky's 40 Comedian Dogs staged village scenes and daily "human life" performed by the "actors"- the dogs. Americans poured in, year on year, comedy juggler WC Fields controlled the stage, while opera singers gave pleasure, and Galetti's Monkeys monopolised mayhem. Irving Berlin's Alexander's Ragtime Band music was all the rage, and from over the Atlantic came the Two Bobs pioneering ragtime in Britain, the Three Ragtime Boys, and Mignonette Kokin the original "turkey-hop girl."

(below)

HG Pelissier, Andre Charlot, Albert De Courville, CB Cochran

(right)

The Whip Race

Revues became the vogue. Fast, free-flowing fun for all. America's new music ragtime evolved to jazz, the Harlem One-Step and its variations gave the Foxtrot and the Quickstep, while Argentina exported the Tango. Ragtime revues headed by Americans - one revue even called *Le Petit Cabaret* - showed the way. "*What Ho! Ragtime*", often staged, was "A delicious slice of American Life." Revues from Paris jostled with British revues. The revue *And Very Nice Too!* had a special matinee in 1913 for the Olympic Games Fund. One Glasgow weekly commented:

> All the world of theatres is mad, happily mad, upon the revue, the
> merry mixture of musical-comedy, farce and music-hall turns
> possessing the advantages of all three and the worries of none.

One opening act was by the Imperial Russian Ballet, which was touring

Europe directed by Diaghilev, performing *Scherazade* by Rimsky Korsakov, the oriental ballet about the sultana Scherazade who saved her life by entertaining her lord with Tales of the Arabian Night. Another week there were racehorses, lady bookmakers, Society women and heavy swells in the *Flyaway Derby* which had a race on the same lines as Ben Hur.

(above) Galetti's Monkeys

(right) WC Fields, Mignonette Kokin, Phyliss Dare and George Grossmith, Ellaline Terry, Jack Buchanan

Irving Berlin and Wylie-Tate Revues

Julian Wylie, an accountant-turned-theatrical agent, and lyricist James Tate joined forces, creating Wylie-Tate revues, follies and pantomimes in many cities. The Alhambra's first was in 1913 - *I Should Worry* - containing ragtime melodies, burlesque and parodies was retained over Christmas. Percy Honri and his big Tango Revue *What About It* was in seven elaborate scenes including the Tea Time Tango. The Bur-Revue-Lesque *A Mixed Grill* in 1914 included a newcomer called Jack Buchanan.

Watch Your Step presented by CB Cochran in 1915 was the first major syncopated musical revue, and the first of many by Irving Berlin. Originally produced in New York, by a son of Glasgow, RH Burnside, its songs included Play a Simple Melody. Louis Mitchell, Harlem's top "rag" drummer and bandoline player was encouraged by Berlin to visit Europe, which he did in 1914 to London, claiming to be "the first man to bring jazz to Britain." In each of the next three years he played the Alhambra with his Syncopating Sextette, before starting his own jazz club in Paris.

From Top to Toe

Other topliners included the French clowns - Continental Musical Comedians - Antonette & Grock who first visited Britain in June 1912, coming the same month to the Alhambra. Grock came again many times with varying partners, whose names got smaller and then dropped off the bill. Nellie Wallace, female comedian "with an uncopiable style, has most amusing ditties with the Hobble and the Harem skirts." Comedy duo Naughton and Gold – better known as Rotten & McNaughton; American comedian RG Knowles, Barclay Gammon

monologuist at the piano who would satirise von Pachmann, the world's greatest pianist; Lily Langtry in one act plays; Princess Bariatinsky in musical comedy; Florence Smithson actress and singer from Wales with the purist high Ds and E's.

Glasgow's Margaret Moffat, comedienne, and Nat D Ayer at the piano in *A Little Entertainment* had a major touring success. Ayer settled from America and was Britain's most popular songwriter, including Oh, You Beautiful Doll, You're My Baby Now, and If You Were the Only Girl in the World (And I was The Only Boy) a lasting favourite of many, including my grandmother.

The impersonator Mlle Fregolia from France was a quick change artiste – making 50 changes of costume in an hour, while performing characters in a solo play. Large turns included Eustace Gray's Palladium Minstrels and the Cigarette Banjo Band of 90 blacked faced artistes, featuring banjo soloist Joe Morley. The theatre staged programmes by the Glasgow Select Choir, and a week of afternoons showing a series of films of "Nature's Zoo" by Cherry Kearton.

Promotion and Profits

Butt's new formula of entertainment, and the splendid new building and luxurious seating, outclassed its competitors. The Alhambra company made profits from year one, and by 1916 its profits were greater than all of the four Howard & Wyndham theatres in Glasgow and Edinburgh put together. For its opening years the theatre's stylish programme cover was designed by book illustrator EP Kinsella. His later poster work included huge billboards of a dancing couple advertising the new Plaza ballroom at Eglinton Toll, before moving to America's film industry.

The theatre sold confectionery, including Agnews Chocolates, teas and

squashes while the bars had White Horse Whisky, Niblick Whisky, Tennent's Lager and Munich Baby Bottles (the coming war changed this to Tennent's British Lager); and Carlsberg Lager in pints and splits (this would change to Genuine Danish Lager.)

Oceans and Empires

Meanwhile Moss Empires continued to expand their interests by starting the first circuit of *vaudeville on the ocean*, adding musical comedy and opera. Britain had the largest shipping lines and encircled the world. Cunard signed a deal to be first and work was completed at Clydebank on board the new liner Aquitania before its maiden voyage in May 1914. The purpose built theatre held 1,500 and had an orchestra, box office, full stage and dressing rooms, to end old style ships concerts in lounges.

Butt had not thought of this but would turn to America for his next big step. However it would take longer than anyone imagined as troops scurried off and naval ships assembled. In newspaper adverts for each week's main feature the Alhambra added the line VARIETIES AND WAR PICTURES.

(above)
RMS Aquitania, Aquitania's Theatre, Florence Smithson, RG Knowles, Nat D Ayer

(opposite)
Julian Wylie and James Tate, Charlot revue - railway porters scene, Kill That Fly revue, Naughton & Gold

The GREAT CARMO
The Colossus of Mystery
By Val Andrews

THE ALHAMBRA
6.45 TWICE NIGHTLY 9 P.M.

Managing Director
Mr ALFRED BUTT

General Manager
Mr JOSEPH WILSON

PROGRAMME

A MAGNIFICENT and PERFECTLY EQUIPPED VARIETY THEATRE

Presenting at all times the BEST of EUROPEAN and AMERICAN VAUDEVILLE ATTRACTIONS

SALOME

I'D STARVE FIRST!

Harry Lauder

In his Stirring Patriotic Song
"THE LADDIES WHO HAVE FOUGHT AND WON"
(At the Shaftesbury Theatre, London)

Glasgow Alhambra

MANAGING DIRECTOR, ... ALFRED BUTT

Presenting at all times the best of European and American Vaudeville Attractions

Programme

WEEK COMMENCING MONDAY, 7th JULY, 1919

MATINEE EVERY WEDNESDAY AT 2-30

1 **OVERTURE**—March, "Tabasco,"   *G. W. Chadwick*

2 **ETHEL LEVEY**   The Famous Anglo-American Star
IN SELECTIONS FROM HER REPERTOIRE.

3 **ERNIE REAM**   And a Baby Grand

4 **ALICE CRAVEN**   The Lancashire Lass

5 **CISSIE LUPINO**   Dancer

6 **ORCHESTRAL INTERLUDE**
Valse, "Caprice,"   *Rubinstein*

7 **DU CALION**   The Loquacious Laddie on the Tottering Ladder

8 **VANWY CHARD**   The Welsh Songstress

9 **HARRY & FRED NAMBA**   Eccentric Entertainers

FROM THE LONDON COLISEUM.   A WONDER ATTRACTION.
10 **ZOMA**   The Psychic Phenomenon
The Woman who can tell you anything. ZOMAH has baffled the Scientists of two Hemispheres. Her brain has been sold to the Doctors.

NEXT WEEK   BOOK EARLY
FELICE LYNE
AND FULL STAR VARIETY PROGRAMME

The order and composition of this Programme may be varied as circumstances require.

ADVANCE BOOKING OFFICE at 99 HOPE STREET.   PHONES—Central 5346-5347.
Seats Booked by 'Phone will be sold unless paid for not later than fifteen minutes before the advertised time of the rise of the Curtain.

Physicians and others expecting a message should leave their names and seat number at the Box Office in Vestibule.   Articles lost or found should be reported to the Office.

THEATRE TELEPHONE NOS.—Central 4690-4691.

Ladies and Gentlemen occupying Seats in Fauteuils and Stalls are respectfully requested to remove their hats. Tickets are sold subject to the observance of this condition.

THE REFRESHMENT BARS ARE OPEN UNTIL 10 P.M.

General Manager,   - - - - -   E. W. CROSSLEY TAYLOR
Acting Manager,   - - - - -   J. H. GERALD
Musical Director,   - - - - -   HOWARD CROFT
Stage Manager,   - - - - -   G. RATCLIFFE

Great War and New Pantomimes

The Alhambra revelled in revues and variety. Patriotic as ever, Alfred Butt staged a grand ballet after war was declared in 1914 entitled *Europe*, with ballerinas representing each of France, Europe, Russia and Britain, supported by the Empire Corps de Ballet.

The second scene was set as a huge raised map of Europe, built of wood, and from doors in it came the dancer representing that nation.

Appearing in Scotland for the first time were Lydia Kyasht and her corps de ballet from Russia, followed at the first Christmas by Russian dancers led by Nidia Nicolayeva and her husband Nicolas Legat, Chef de Ballet of the Russian Imperial Ballet at Petrograd. Among his many students would be Mona Inglesby and Moira Shearer. Sarah Bernhardt played her new one act drama *Du Theatre au Champ d'Honneur* - "as if Bernhardt came to us with the smoke of the battlefields still clinging about her." The Covent Garden company's opera *Samson & Delilah* was led by contralto diva Kirkby Lunn. All followed by variety.

Harry Lauder

Britain's best known entertainer now came to the Alhambra, in 1915. Harry Lauder, supported by Nellie Wallace, "the Quintessence of Quaintness", and the band of the Argyll & Sutherland Highlanders, was raising money for the Relief Fund for Disabled Soldiers before a world tour to raise support for Britain's War Effort. Seat prices went up.

The Harry Lauder postcard, The Laddies who have Fought and Won, was one of a series of 500 performers whose photocards were sold in vast numbers "for the benefit of the brave men-at-the-Front. The money received is devoted to sending 1/- parcels (really 3/6d worth) of tobacco and cigarettes through "The Performer" Tobacco Fund. One card is enclosed in each parcel to liven up a Dug-out." One of the theatre's charity shows was for the Belgian Red Cross, with singers and pianists from Belgian theatres; another for the Lord Provost's Prisoner of War Fund for those incarcerated in Germany.

Ethel Levey lights the way

American comedienne and actress Ethel Levey took centre stage - "the most extensively gowned woman on the variety stage, ragtime and dance." The songs Yankee Doodle Dandy and Give My Regards to Broadway were specially written for her.

Headliners continued such as Maud Allan, Vesta Tilley now in khaki

(above)
Ethel Levey
Opposite
(left)
The Great Carmo
Lydia Kyasht
Cartoon
(centre)
Harry Lauder and soldiers
Lauder arrives in New York
Lauder postcard
1919 Programme

singing "The Army of Today's All Right" (but the lions were being led by donkeys, and too many did not return), Fred Karno, Lily Langtry, Grock who could have become a resident of Glasgow, Adeline Genee, David Devant,

(left)

Cecilia Loftus, Ella Retford, Neil Kenyon, Scott & Whaley, Alice Delysia

impressionist Cecilia Loftus, raven-haired Gertie Gitana, the Forces Sweetheart with the signature tune Nellie Dean, the alluring Alice Delysia from the Moulin Rouge who sang the original Noel Coward song Poor Little Rich Girl–and became the Desert Army's favourite trouper in the next War; comedian Neil Kenyon (from Greenock), the entertaining Lupino clan, the first black American comedians in Britain, Scott & Whaley; GS Melvin, Wee Georgie Wood; and George T Pattman, of the Royal College of Organists, organist for a time at St Mary's Cathedral, Glasgow, playing selections on a £3,000 organ containing over 1,000 pipes, accompanied by a lady singer. The organ is now in Durham School Chapel.

In August 1916 actress Lena Ashwell brought her Firing Line Concert Party giving their entertainment "exactly as they carried it right up to the firing line where they performed to upwards of 30,000 men either coming out or going into the trenches". Plays continued with the Moffat Family, Ellen Terry, Shakespeare by Sir Frank Benson, new writings by JM Barrie and JJ Bell. A play of life at the Front by cartoonist Captain Bruce Bairnsfather – *The Better 'Ole* – described the real thing in humour and irony. He also drew sketches which were shown by magic lantern during the overture.

Andre Charlot - Master of Revue

The Master of Revue was Andre Charlot who relied on elegance and simplicity. He described his revues as "small, intimate and absolutely connected." He avoided spectacular settings. His actors were expected to work, making countless changes each performance. He nurtured his discoveries including Beatrice Lillie, Jack Buchanan, Gertrude Lawrence, Binnie Hale, Jessie Matthews and Noel Coward. Oscar Ashe appeared in *Hajj*, his own revised edition of *Kismet*.

Wylie-Tate and Alfred Butt started an annual series of long lavish revues, with no variety following, which took their name, *The Passing Show* from America, where they became the Zeigfeld revues. The first in the Alhambra opened with 65 artistes in 1915 starring Ella Retford, remembered for her song I Was a Good Little Girl Till I Met You.

However, even more men were needed for the Services and war production. In 1917 Neville Chamberlain, Director of National Service, declared that "there could be reductions in the labour employed on stage mechanical devices and the making of expensive costumes to free more people for war work." He also said "The amusement of the people is an essential part of national work." Alfred Butt replied saying that the theatre companies would consider reducing the numbers drastically in productions.

Lions and elephants

Australia's Wonder, the Great Carmo, staged spectaculars featuring comedy sharpshooting, sketches, impersonations, music and magic. His latest sensation, *The Vanishing Lion*, packed the house – to witness a full grown lion disappear in full view of the audience from an open cage. Lockhart's Famous Elephants were truly famous and were stabled nearby. Every night for their week they marched through the streets to the theatre. On a smaller scale the Van Camp Pigs had attendant canaries introducing a boxing bout between two little pigs.

The annual touring pantomimes included *The Forty Thieves* starring Jimmy Learmouth. It had 15 principals, 40 thieves, 4 dancers, 6 gents singers, and 2 camels.

The last in the theatre, in 1916, was *Cinderella* with Scotch Kelly as Billy Buttons, "a Ballet of Irish Beauties, Gorgeous Scenery, Electric Coach and Real Shetland Ponies".

Wylie-Tate Pantomimes

The Alhambra started full seasons of Wylie-Tate pantomimes with *Dick Whittington* in 1917/18, featuring Ella Retford and Harry Weldon who had been in Fred Karno's army as Stiffy the Goalie. The Glasgow Herald noted:

(right)

Lena Ashwell, A Better 'Ole, Captain Bruce Bairnsfather, Pamela songsheet with Lily Elsie, The Six Brown Brothers

> Enterprising vaudeville managers have not stopped at producing full-length plays. It is no surprise to see the pantomime season in Glasgow inaugurated on the music-hall stage on a more ambitious scale. Even the baggy trousered knave who once sported with Harlequinade makes his bow before the rise of the curtain.

The next year, Wylie-Tate's *Jack and the Beanstalk* premiered at the Alhambra with Dorothy Ward as Jack and her real-life husband Shaun Glenville as the Dame. The 100 performers included the Pender Troupe of

Pantomimists, who came often and included Archie Leach from Bristol, the future Cary Grant. Wylie used the best costume designers, this year includ-

ing Marcelle de Saint Martin for a, very French, Plum Pudding Ballet, and in next year's *Passing Show* she and Dolly Tree designed a vocal ballet My Lady Liquor and the American Cocktails. Prohibition was starting.

The premiere of CB Cochran's romantic comedy *Cyrano de Bergerac* featuring Robert Loraine and Lewis Casson confirmed Alhambra's status as a major theatre, under the direction of new manager Crossley Taylor.

Sir Alfred Butt's Invitations to VCs

In 1919 Sir Alfred Butt issued his "Invitations to VCs" to all living holders of the Victoria Cross – World War 1 and pre-war – and presented medallions to about 500 men, giving them free access to any of the theatres he controlled. The Sir Alfred Butt medallions are silver-gilt on a link to be worn with a chain watch, and are inscribed with the holder's name. 1919 could start to be normal.

During the Great War Alfred Butt knew that films had become more important, for news and relaxation, and he commissioned film-makers to go to Gallipoli and record what was happening. Despite family pressure Sir Alfred Butt declined to be chairman of a syndicate which be-

(above)

The Pender Troupe, Oscar Asche as Hajj, Dorothy Ward in pantomime, Cary Grant

(right)

Programme adverts

came the Alliance Film Company formed in 1919 to produce films from new studios to be built near Hendon. It planned to be the largest in the world, capable of producing six films simultaneously, and aimed to compete with

Sir Alfred Butt Director of Food Rationing

During the war Alfred Butt presented variety entertainment at Buckingham Palace on special occasions, including three days in 1916 for wounded soldiers. Tea was "served by members of the Royal Family and Society." He became a candidate for Parliament and because of his business prowess he was supported by newspaper baron Lord Northcliffe. Britain was losing the war, was bankrupt, and now faced starvation as Germany announced its U-Boats would sink any ships approaching Britain.

The vacillating Asquith was replaced by David Lloyd George as Prime Minister at the end of 1916, improving war production, instantly starting the convoy system for merchant ships to give a better chance of survival, and making food rationing compulsory for the first time in Britain. At Northcliffe's suggestion he made Alfred Butt the Director of Food Rationing. The previous voluntary system, covering few items, had failed. Butt made certain the new system worked. Helped by his civil servant, William Beveridge (of later Health & Welfare note), the ration books with separate coloured leaves for various foods, were controlled on a regional basis. Butt delegated well, and always engaged able lieutenants. He was knighted in 1918 for his services to the Ministry of Food.

(above)

Sir Alfred Butt
Medallion for VC
holders

A volunteer official, Mrs Peel, published her memoirs commenting on how people had to do different things:

"Sir Alfred Butt, who did such good work in regard to compulsory rationing, was another of these "quick-change artists." Why his great knowledge of matters theatrical should have fitted him to deal with compulsory rationing I cannot tell. I only know that he once, with his second-in-command, came down with me to the Westminster Bridge Kitchen, where I was greatly struck with his evident love for children, his interest in those who were buying their dinners, and his delight that instead of being obliged to dine off pieces of bread they could now go to the public kitchen and buy for a few pence a nourishing substantial meal.

It was one of the jokes of the Ministry of Food that Sir Alfred had brought his theatrical choruses along with him in the guise of clerks and typists, and certainly the appearance of some of the young ladies who tripped in and out of his office in Park Street would not have disgraced the front row of any ballet."

American imports. Instead Sir Water de Frece became chairman, and the Company sagged.

Butt preferred new challenges on stage. In Britain repertory theatre was alive, involving new people, writers, and topics. In America new large scale musicals were being thought of, matching the energy and colour of Zeigfeld's Follies.

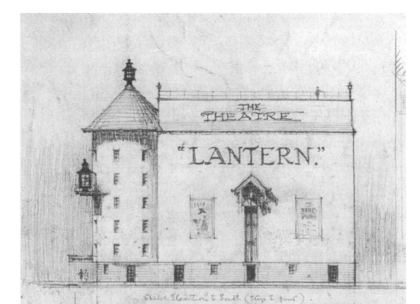

A Second Theatre?

Sir Alfred Butt, chairman of the Alhambra, "proposes to form a new company to build a theatre on the north-east corner of Wellington Street and Waterloo Street. Sir John Burnett has prepared plans which show a first-class theatre could be created on the site chosen."

The newspapers purred with anticipation. He addressed the company - "I have no hesitation in saying that the position occupied by the Glasgow Alhambra is unsurpassed by that of any theatre in the country. But in this respect I should remind all concerned - not only those associated with the Glasgow Alhambra but with the industry in general – that there is a limit to the holding capacity and consequent takings of a place of entertainment, and that it is necessary that we should all remember the fate of the goose and the golden eggs."

Flying the Stars and Stripes

1919 was a busy year in Glasgow, London and Paris. Alhambra's profits continued to rise, and shareholders got dividends of 40%. In January, Butt, with the immense financial backing of Solly Joel, emerged as the victor in a takeover battle for London's Theatre Royal, Drury Lane. Three years later it opened with a remodelled auditorium, although remaining much smaller than the Alhambra, and he now brought to Britain new American musicals. It was noted that "he did everything short of flying the Stars and Stripes over Drury Lane."

Vive la France

In the summer of 1919 his newly built Paris Palace Theatre opened, running for five years, until changing its name to the Mogador Theatre under new owners. It was built specially for his mistress the glamorous French dancer and singer Regine Flory – who starred at its opening night attended by many notables in the city for the final signing of the Peace Treaty, including President Woodrow Wilson as principal guest, Lord Derby and Baron Rothschild. Regine Flory led seven major shows of Alfred Butt in Britain, USA and France until new musicals for her became scarcer. Curiously she turned down the leading role in *No, No, Nanette* –which set the international benchmark for musicals. Sadly in 1926, after travelling from Paris to London, she shot herself in front of Sir Alfred in his Drury Lane office when he told her there were still no parts for her.

(above)
Regine Flory
(opposite)
The Lantern Theatre
Waterloo Street Bus Station

Songsheets

Alliance with Moss Empires

In October of 1919 Butt sold his interest in the declining Variety Theatres Controlling Company combine to Moss Empires, who kept some of the music-halls but demolished most or changed them to picture houses. Glasgow Alhambra Ltd continued to be an independent business, and decided to have as joint managing directors – RH Gillespie, a managing director of Moss Empires, and Sir Alfred Butt who was also now the Alhambra's chairman. At this point they also appointed as a director John Wishart of Lancaster Gate, Glasgow, a director of major rubber, oil and plantation companies, and of Moss Empires Ltd. His daughter married Victor Warren, a future Lord Provost of the city.

(above)
RH Gillespie

At the Alhambra, Butt's new general manager Crossley Taylor, who rose to the rank of Captain during the war, set the tone for the coming decades. As well as advising the board on the selection of shows to be staged and immaculately managing and publicising the house he ensured his stars featured in the promotions of fashion shops, stores, motor showrooms, newspapers and radio; exhibitions at the Kelvin Hall; sports events; and gala dances at the Plaza Ballroom, and at Dennistoun Palais de Danse. He even organised the first cabaret in Glasgow. In 1924 he started a glossy monthly illustrated magazine printed by Moss Empires, the *Alhambra Tatler*, with show news, running until 1940 when wartime's shortage of paper stopped many things.

At the annual meeting of the company in December 1919 Butt broke the good news of his plans for a second theatre, to be built across from the Alhambra.

Repertory movements

From 1918 architect James Salmon was sketching outline drawings for a theatre for the Scottish Repertory Company Ltd – which started a decade before as the Scottish Playgoers Ltd, partly supported by Howard & Wyndham. He examined sites mainly around Bothwell Street, drafted specifications and made financial comparisons to existing theatres in Glasgow and London. The proposed new theatre, to be called The Lantern, would accommodate 1400 on three levels, all connected by elevator; be air conditioned, with plans for roof gardens; the stage would be capable of being raised and lowered in sections, and a rehearsal stage would be provided. Club facilities would include accommodation and garaging.

Sir Alfred Butt's statement

Butt's statement continued- "It came to my knowledge that certain other people (the Scottish Repertory Company) were endeavouring to secure the excellent site which virtually faces this theatre, for the purpose of another place of entertainment. This would be prejudicial to the interests of this company for this site to be acquired by third parties, and accordingly I have purchased the site.

"I propose to form a new and separate company to develop this site for a really high-class theatre. Alhambra shareholders would have preferential rights in subscribing for some of its shares.

The theatre I propose to erect will not, in my opinion, interfere or enter into direct competition with those already existing. It will be of a much more ambitious theatre, and will be equipped in such a manner as to enable Glasgow, with its population of over a million, from time to time to produce original plays, and thereafter send them broadcast all over the English-speaking world, instead of always receiving plays which have been produced by myself and other managers, either in London or New York, for their premieres.

The new theatre will also be equipped to enable Glasgow to enjoy all that is best in high-class music and opera. I am not at liberty at the moment to mention the name of the proposed theatre but I hope when you all hear it, which I think you will do so shortly, the title in itself will be in accordance with our ambitions."

The Baillie magazine enthused:

> Here in the West of Scotland we are seeing a revival of Music, the elder sister of the Arts. The Repertory Theatre movement has been a clear manifestation of the craving for better things. Sir Alfred Butt has sensed the situation, and his orientation is welcome.

Money in the coffers

During 1920 the company reregistered and trebled in size financially. Moss Empires invested in 20% of the enlarged company at a cost of £21,000, which came from selling the Metropole in Stockwell Street to Glasgow impresario Bernard Frutin. However at the 1921 annual company meeting Butt announced that "owing to industrial conditions ….. I do not feel justified in embarking upon a scheme which I know must involve a greater amount of capital than I had previously anticipated." Unfortunately Burnet's drawings did not survive the next war. Instead the continuing profits and new shares would be used for a major extension of the Alhambra starting in 1927. Sir Alfred continued to own the second site for a few years until it was developed as Waterloo Street Bus Station in 1927.

(top left)

Taxi Stance at Waterloo Street by Robert Eadie RSW

(above)

Songsheets

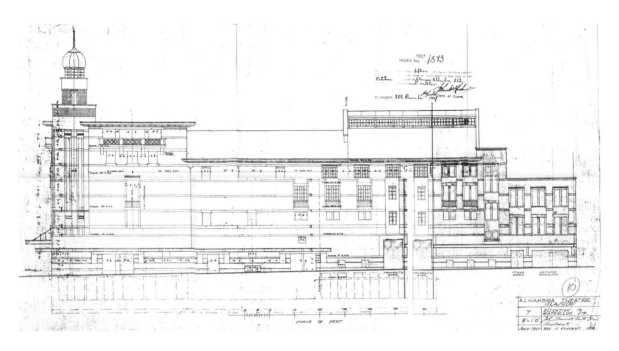

Roaring Twenties and No, No, Nanette

Alhambra's bill of fare packed the house twice nightly, to the delight of audiences and shareholders. The attraction of a headliner, revue, ballet or play, followed by variety acts proved unbeatable.If there was a long revue or play, followed by variety, the complete show changed to being once nightly. Where variety led, it was sometimes followed by repertory plays after the interlude. At the 1921 annual company meeting Sir Alfred voiced the need for new ideas:

> With music-hall artistes on lengthy contracts at increased salaries
> the incentive to provide themselves with new acts, new songs
> and other materials to attract the public has disappeared.

Revues

Revues ran for 1-3 weeks each. The annual *Passing Shows* were once nightly. More shows kept opening - *Midnight Frolics* with Gertrude Lawrence, *Hello America!, Bran Pie, The Follies*- often with the Lupino family, *The Bing Boys on Broadway, Honi Soit, The New Bran Pie, The Scrap Book, A to Z* designed by Dolly Tree, and led by Jack Buchanan, who created the dance routines, and sang one

of Ivor Novello's earliest songs And Her Mother Came Too, *The Peep Show* designed each year by Dolly Tree, *Pot Luck* with Cicely Courtneidge and Jack Hulbert, *Airs and Breezes, Fun of the Fayre, Kippers & Kings* by Glasgow actor and producer Robert Courtneidge (father of Cicely) featured Peggy O'Neill, *Phi-Phi, Dancing Mad*, and many more. The *Manhattan Follies* - directly from Manhattan - was in "twenty sparkling scenelets," and *The Pepper Box* by Tom Arnold had 30 scenes.

Splinters came, being the all male First Army Entertainers, known also as Les Rouge et Noirs on account of their regimental colours, who started at the Front in 1917. *The Garden of Allah* by Wylie-Tate was alive with camels, mules, monkeys, sheep and goats. *A (K)night in Venice* opened with Will Fyffe and Ida Crispi whose "songs will haunt the ear, and make the milk boy melodious on the coldest morning." The pierrotic entertainment of *The Co-optimists* led by Laddie Cliff for five summer seasons had changes weekly, and gave a start to Stanley Holloway and Tommy Handley.

(above)
Revue Costumes
Gertrude Lawrence
(opposite)
Alhambra extension westward

Alhambra Tatler covers for Sunny, Desert Song, The New Moon Songsheets

Variety artistes

Audiences enjoyed a cornucopia - Sir Harry Lauder, Harry Tate, Grock, co-medienne Ethel Levey with the support of the Plassket Jazz Band, Nat D Ayer, syncopated singer Norah Bayes, who made popular Shine On, Harvest

Moon and Over There (The Yanks Are Coming) which entertained America's troops during the war, Gaby Deslys, prima donna Florence Smithson, George Robey, GH Elliot including his latest song success California, impersonator Hetty King, organist GT Pattman, Nervo and Knox, Naughton & Gold, illusionist De Biere, the high-stepping Dolly Sisters, the Trix Sisters of high speed ragtime – who started a cabaret club in Paris - the guitar playing Duncan Sisters, and also from America Sophie Tucker, described as "Everybody's Pal". She was a solo artist unlike "the very peppy and hot-ziggety" singing sisters. She had

(above)

Costumes for A-Z Chorus, GH Elliot, Gaby Deslys, George Robey

a new gimmick for the Alhambra – two accompanists on two pianos, and a new kind of song in which it wasn't sisters she was looking for. Her songs included One of These Days, You're Going To Miss Me Honey.

Grock's appeal, as with all the greatest comedians, was not so much what he did as how he did it. The look of catastrophe when he discovered that sitting on the stool he could not reach the piano – the pondering of the problem – the dawning look of triumph as he was suddenly struck by the solution – to shove the piano over to the stool. Fred Karno & Co included Will Hay and Glasgow's Billy Bennet. Sketches in Karno's Revue of 1922 caught a reporter's eye:

> The hapless manager of a hire furniture shop, attempts to sell a happy
> home to a bashful honeymoon couple. Another novel scene is of
> a garage with five motor cars, each with a mascot. In the stillness
> of the night the mascots come to life and perform a goblin dance.
> "Classes and Masses" is a topical skit on the housing question.

One of the first Chinese entertainers gaining international celebrity was Long Tack Sam. and his magnificently dressed Troupe of jugglers, balancers, contortionists and magicians, the equal of Cirque d'Soleil today. Bert Levy, the Australian artist and entertainer, always gave a musical matinee for 200 poorer children, telling stories, drawing rapid and vigorous cartoons projected on a screen which he animated including the Playful Dynosaurus, and throwing it apples which it consumed.

Singer and dancer Jenny Golder from Australia via the Folies Bergeres made her debut in Scotland – singing in French, English, Spanish and Italian. "Between each song she is seen in silhouette dressing behind a screen that is lit from the back. In her final song she has an ingenious pierrot dress which in the darkness shines with a phosphorous glow."

The popular Julien Rose, acting as Levinsky, related a story about a firm of profiteers – "the two partners of the firm had done very well out of the war but things were beginning to look black, so one partner suggested that now the good times were over, a little honest business might not come amiss. "No, no" replied the other partner, "I never indulge in experiments." The Sheffield Choir enjoyed top billing under Dr Henry Coward who was reviving choral singing across Britain.

Specialties and Samoiloff

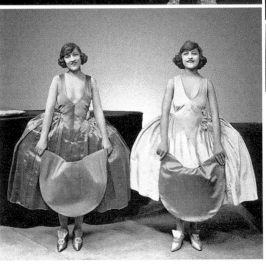

The graceful swimmer and diver Odiva brought her school of Pacific Sea Lions and got waves of applause. The Circus Queen was a touring spectacle, in seven scenes, including an actual horse race and a complete Circus on stage. Psychics impressed, with Mercedes being described as the Eighth Wonder of the World accompanied by Miss Stantone on the piano – "Joe Mercedes transfers in silence and sincerity by telepathic waves to Miss Stantone any musical selections suggested by the audience from Grand Opera to Ragtime."

The Man with Two Brains enjoyed juggling with figures. M. Jacques Inaudi

(above)

The Dolly Sisters,
The Trix Sisters,
Sophie Tucker,
Grock, Long Tack
Sam, Bert Levy

"is a mental acrobatist, while conversing with the audience he calculates the answers to mathematical questions posed to him, for example a request for the fifth root of 14,359,707 – the answer "27" was given with very little delay." He out-calculated professors at the Sorbonne. America's Leona La Mar -The Girl with a Thousand Eyes - "demonstrates thought transference when blindfolded, describing the appearance of a person and telling them events of their life, past, present and future and answering all sorts of questions from the audience." Pressmen were loathe to interview her!

(below)
Jenny Golder, Jose Collins, Little Nellie Kelly, Peggy O'Neill, Jacques Inaudi being tested on stage by reporters

Puppetry included Delvaine's Marionettes, Schistte's Comical Wonderettes from America, and the Marionette Players from Rome's Teatro del Picoli who

had 10 operators, 100 stage settings available and over 500 marionettes. From 1923 the Bioscope included an animated cartoon starting with Tishy (the cross–legged horse).

Russian émigré Adrian Samoiloff staged Magic & Light acts, splitting and moving rays, and was often used in revues. Before

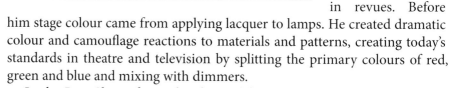

him stage colour came from applying lacquer to lamps. He created dramatic colour and camouflage reactions to materials and patterns, creating today's standards in theatre and television by splitting the primary colours of red, green and blue and mixing with dimmers.

In the *Peep Show* of 1922 he changed four scenes completely without removing the costumes and scenery. The Valley of the Echoes, silent hills and valley, disappear and become a vast ancient Hall of Egypt. A black man becomes white and the gorgeous apparel of an Indian Rajah becomes a modern lounge suit. An old woman of 60 changes to a girl of 16. A table piled with books becomes a money bank. A dress changes not only in colour but in pattern and shape, being high in the neck in one light and décolleté in another.

Musicals & plays

In the early Twenties musicals included Jose Collins in *Maid of the Mountain*, produced by Oscar Asche, staged once nightly; *The Street Singer* with Phyllis Dare, and the toe tapping *Little Nellie Kelly*, with Sonnie Hale. Appearing in many musicals and revues, the Irish-American singer and actress Peggy O'Neill was a qualified air pilot who often flew to her city theatre destinations.

Seasons of new plays, and favourites, by Graham Moffat were joined by new Sherlock Holmes adventures by A Conan Doyle, all followed by variety. Sir Johnston Forbes-Robertson recited Shakespeare. Peggy O'Neill led in JM Barrie's *What Every Woman Wants*. *White Cargo*, *Mercenary Mary* and the *Green Goddess* became regular plays, as did Matheson Lang in *The Chinese Bungalow*. Plays by George Bernard Shaw brought lengthy queues at the Hope Street box office. Repertory weeks included three weeks by Mrs Patrick Campbell, seasons by the Irish Players, the Scottish National Players, and the later arrival of the Ardrossan & Saltcoats Players.

A three week season of the Olga Katzin & Hugh Miller Repertory Company featured many Scots actors from previous repertories. The last week was *Wurzle-Flummery* by AA Milne who had written for Butt before. Bransby Williams famous for Charles Dickens studies impersonated characters in *David Copperfield* at the drop of a wig, and the next week *Oliver Twist*, and so on. But he got his biggest applause by appearing as Lloyd George and making a fighting speech. *The Rat*, once nightly, starred its author Ivor Novello – actor, film heart throb, and composer. The *Broken Wing*, also once nightly, staged a sensational air-crash.

(above)

Maud Allan visits the creche at the Housing Exhibition, Kelvin Hall. The Marion Morgan Company, Graham Moffat Comedies flyer, Matheson Lang as Mr Wu, Ivor Novello

Dance & ballet

Maud Allan commanded full houses. One season in 1922 she kicked off the football game at Shawfield between Scotland Ladies and England Ladies, but

(below)

Leonide Massine and dancers, Mossbank Industrial School and its band wait to enter. At the top of the Beanstalk.

the visitors won. Anna Pavlova now added the Alhambra to her Glasgow venues, and in 1923 members of the Marion Morgan Company of classical dancers, presenting the ballet-play *Helen of Troy* the week before, delayed their return to America in order to see Pavlova perform. Leonide Massine, who danced and choreographed many revues, became a regular with his own dancers from the Imperial Russian Ballet.

Tamara Karsavina, former principal artiste of the Imperial Russian Ballet

in St Petrograd, performed with her corps de ballet. Her pupils included Alicia Markova and Margot Fonteyn. Alhambra hosted Bac and Konami Ishii, the first Japanese ballet dancers appearing in Britain.

Pantomime bouquets and bottles

At the finale of *Mother Goose* in 1922 the Evening Times wrote of:

Bouquets of flowers, baskets of fruit and boxes of chocolate from ardent admirers extended in a line across the Alhambra stage and were handed over the footlights to Miss Dorothy Ward last night who announced the gifts would delight the youngsters of the Sick Children's Hospital, Yorkhill. During the war bouquets were declared "off" on principles of national economy.

Journalist Jack House recalls his favourite pantomime, *The Queen of Hearts*, with Lupino Lane as the Knave,:

Lupino Lane's big scene was his trap-door act when he flashed in and out of 80 trap doors from the stage to the top of the scenery, occupying the whole of the proscenium , like the front of a block of flats with doors on various levels. Lane performed the most amazing

acrobatics with a team of French trap-door specialists. Its *raison-d'etre* in the pantomime was that the Knave was being pursued by the secret police to bring him to justice for his misdeeds.

The way the five of them hurled themselves in and out of the myriad doors baffles description. Lane was always eluding his pursuers by a hairsbreadth, and you never knew on which level he would next appear. The timing was perfection and, of course, Lane escaped and the chase ended. Even in the Moscow State Circus I have never seen anything like it. I saw it many times and on its last night he excelled himself. Just as it was rushing to its climax, he presented each of the French performers, in turn and with perfect timing, with a bottle of whisky as a farewell present.

For *Jack & the Beanstalk* opening in 1923 there were 100 men employed arranging the stage. And the programme encouraged patrons to VOTE AGAINST Britain adopting the Prohibition of alcohol, which American had. The first paragraph read "ALHAMBRA - what glory this conveys" and the second read "PROHIBITION - what misery this conveys." Britain avoided Prohibition but allowed local Veto Polls, which many communities adopted to go dry or restrict the numbers of licences.

Firsts on the Airwaves

Weeks before the BBC started, the first theatrical broadcasters in Scotland were Lupino Lane and Mona Vivien of the Alhambra in January 1923. Coinciding with the

(above)

Dolly Tree, Harry Welchman and Lupino Lane, Mona Vivien, Evelyn Laye

Scottish Motor Show the Daimler Company used studios erected by Marconi at Hughenden Road, Kelvinside. From the Daimler Station 2BP they gave a half hour programme early each evening, before their pantomime performances, from 27th January into February. It was heard as far north as Inverness and east in Edinburgh. 2BP also gave recitals, orchestral concerts, recitations, and news bulletins. It was hoped programmes would continue until the opening in March of the first BBC station, Glasgow's 5SC, but ended in February.

Each March BBC welcomed theatre performers to celebrate the birthday of station 5SC, and in 1925 Binnie Hale and George Grossmith broadcast part of Alhambra's operetta *Cinderella* from the BBC studio in Bath Street.

A first for BBC onboard ship

In June 1926 the principals in Alhambra's musical comedy *Betty in Mayfair* starring Evelyn Laye, assisted by the ship's orchestra, gave a concert relayed from on board the passenger liner SS California of the Anchor Line, berthed at

Yorkhill Quay. Lines were attached to the ship and the concert took place in the lounge, broadcast live by station 5SC.

Shows by design

Revues and musicals increased, and variety weeks decreased. From 1924 even pantomimes gave way, for the next ten years. The first to replace pantomime was the Wylie-Tate revue *Brighter London* with Ruth French who had danced in Pavlova's Ballet. Its modern glamorous costumes were designed by **Dolly Tree**, who was creating sumptuous costumes for stage

(above)

Costume design by Doris Zinkeisen, Doris Zinkeisen, Sybil Thorndike, Programme covers

and screen in Britain, cabaret in Paris and later in America. She started with Butt as a programme illustrator, becoming his chief costume designer, and for four years was the sole stage designer for Wylie-Tate shows, before becoming a legendary costume designer for Hollywood's film industry, where she also invented the strapless evening gown.

Another leading theatrical designer was **Doris Zinkeisen**. She and her sister Anna were born and brought up in Rosneath on the Clyde and on the family moving to London they blossomed as painters and illustrators, with Doris becoming set and costume designer for CB Cochran's shows – for almost 20 years his chief designer – and for Jack Buchanan, Noel Coward and Howard Wilcox.

Dame Sybil Thorndike

From 1924 Sybil Thorndike, a daughter of Scotland, became a favourite in plays including *The Trojan Women*, and later *Medea* - both translated from ancient Greek by Gilbert Murray, Professor of Greek at Glasgow University. She also made *Joan of Arc*, and *Henry VIII* her own. Accompanied by her husband Lewis Casson she gave orations from plays and poems at a packed meeting of the newly formed Glasgow University Dramatic Society in 1926. After a vote of thanks she said:

> Although Glasgow people are noisy at the intervals they make a beautiful audience when anything is happening. In my opinion the best audiences are to be had in Glasgow, Edinburgh and among the East End Jews of London. They are the only audiences I can ever bank on to be perfectly quiet while the performance is going on.

The manager held some special Saturday matinees including an illustrated talk in 1924 on Luxor and the Tomb of Tutankhamun by Arthur Weigall, set designer and producer. He was previously Chief Inspector of Antiquities in Upper Egypt and coined the phrase the "Curse of the Pharoahs." Other matinees raised money to support the welfare of children, servicemen, and infirmaries including the new Homeopathic Hospital, and notably in 1923 a Sacred Concert for Falkirk's Redding Pit Disaster Relief Fund – when a pit was flooded and 40 coal miners died.

(above)

Arthur Capel's Jazz Band, Cabaret-Souper-Dansant , Nellie Wallace

First Cabaret in Glasgow

On 13th January 1925 under the patronage of Lord and Lady Weir, Julian Wylie presented a *Cabaret-Souper-Dansant* in the Grosvenor Restaurant, Gordon Street, with 50 performers from his revue at the Alhambra and pantomime at the Royal. Proceeds went to the new Ear Nose and Throat Hospital being built. Tickets were 2 guineas, available from the Alhambra manager Crossley Taylor. After the supper, dancing was from 9.30pm with Frank Merton's Grosvenor Orchestra and the cabaret from 11.30pm to 1.30am compered by Nellie Wallace, with Arthur Capel's Jazz Band from the Alhambra. Glasgow had caught up with London's Piccadilly!

The Evening Times wrote about June nights:

These are great nights at the Alhambra with wedding parties in silks and glad attire giving a brilliant appearance to the auditorium. On an evening such as yesterday's one could not help regretting that the custom of donning one's "Sunday best" for the theatre was not more general. All the hues of the rainbow and a few extra ones, devised by the dress makers, were on view. Silk hats and spats were almost in the majority.

The Jazz Mistress

Some weeks reverted to twice nightly variety including a Harry Lauder week in 1925, with the programme indicators going up for each act and the stage hands working even faster. One paper wrote of the week topped by a New Zealander, *The Jazz Mistress*:

If you are a chronic dyspeptic with a hunch for old world melodies and have a downright hatred for "jazz" then shun the Alhambra this week. It is almost too late to warn you for by this time all "jazz" enthusiasts have no doubt had their fill of such rich fare served up in a rollicking style, by 19 year old Miss Winifred Arthur, jazz violinist and vocalist, and her band. This performance is "stirring" in every sense of the word. It racks one, exalts one, dejects one – brings tears of joy and sorrow. If you can leave the Alhambra this week without a desire to "shimmy" down Waterloo Street then you've a sphinx of the stoniest kind. Come to the Alhambra and get loosened out.

(left)

Anchor Liner in Govan Dry Dock, Gordon Street from Hope Street by Robert Eadie RSW, Rose Marie Totem Girl, Carl Brisson

No, No, Nanette

Each year more musicals chose to open in Glasgow, before London, many from across the Atlantic. This latest one, originally produced in Chicago, had new tunes added prior to New York - including I Want to be Happy, and Tea for Tea. For its British premiere the producer was William Mollison Jnr, son of Glasgow, and

No, No, Nanette - A New Age

Even the Alhambra, the scene of so many brilliant premieres, has never known another first night like it. There was in the February weeks of 1925 before the opening a certain amount of excitement in Glasgow. True, the show had been a big success in America – but after all American musicals, even successful ones, were no great novelty in Glasgow. On the evening of February 23 it opened and Glasgow went Nanette-crazy.

The house rose to the show – some people even stood on the seats to cheer higher if not louder – and the audience simply refused to go home until Binnie Hale, Joe Coyne, George Grossmith and the rest of the cast had sung each twinkling tune again and again. Next morning there were block-long queues before the theatre opened – the shops were swamped with orders for sheet music and records. In Glasgow, not to know Nanette was to be socially dead.

(Eddie Ashton)

There were placards in the streets for days saying "Yes, Yes, Nanette". But maybe the biggest stars of the whole show were in the orchestra pit. Glasgow had never heard anything like Percival Mackey and his Band. He had been Jack Hylton's pianist, and was the first to use jazz musicians in pit orchestras. When they played the hit tunes at the interval hardly a soul went to the bar. I should think that the bar drawings at the Alhambra can never have been lower than during *No, No, Nanette*.

The audience would not go home. Next day the Hope Street box office was swamped. In those days there was an organization known as The Glasgow Boy Messenger Service, and you could hire the services of a boy wearing a uniform rather like the Boys Brigade to do such things as standing in a queue for you. There were so many Messenger Boys in Hope Street it looked like a daily military parade. All girls took to wearing Three Yard dresses like Binnie Hale's. They were called that because you needed only three yards of material to make them.

(Jack House)

(above)
Tea for Two songsheet, Binnie Hale, No No Nanette poster

starred George Grossmith and Binnie Hale with all-action dances by two choruses, syncopations and saxophones. A masseur in the wings was essential!

All Advance tickets for the show sold out at the box office leaving only tickets on sale each day for 600 places in the gods. For its last Saturday, queues from 6am grew to over 3,000 – selling out the matinee and evening tickets minutes after the box opened at 10am. There were four queues separated by barriers and those at the back charged to the front. Police reinforcements were called to curb the near-riot. Tickets changed hands for 10 times the face value. Those who gained a gods ticket for the evening queued at the theatre in the afternoon to get a "best view" position. The manager let them in two hours before curtain up and put on films of Charlie Chaplain. Many brought soup flasks and sandwiches.

After that box office melee *all* seats were now made bookable in advance.

Sir Alfred reported to the company that profits had increased by 25% due to the large-scale musicals arranged through the Moss Empires connection.

Rose Marie

Rose Marie romanced in the Rockies with 60 chorus dancers and a male chorus of 30 during a severe flu epidemic, which affected the chorus girls in the

most energetic dance ever seen – the Totem Tom Tom. But each fainting girl managed to get to the side without the audience seeing, and in the wings the St Andrews Ambulance men put them on stretchers.

The Apache revue opened with the flappers' idol Carl Brisson, and Dorothy Ward. Premieres included *Princess Charming*, a successor to *No, No, Nanette*, with Alice Delysia and Eton Crop hairstyles galore; and from the USA came *Tip Toes*, with Dorothy Dickson making Look for The Silver Lining her theme tune, to which she later added These Foolish Things.

Art and commerce

1926 saw more new artistes who became favourites, with the general manager claiming that "the most artistic productions were staged by commercial managements, not the indifferent standards of the civic repertory movement." Nikita Balieff and his *Chauve-Souris* – the Bat Theatre – began their visits. He started in Moscow, moving after 1917 to Paris. One critic described "The World's Most Artistic Revue" as an

(above)

Dorothy Dickson, Nikita Balieff, Ella Logan, Chauve Souris scenes - Russian ballad of Huntsmen, French ballad of Avignon

entertainment more novel, and perhaps, more artistic than anything since Nijinsky and Pavlova. One of his creations was The Parade of the Wooden Soldier - based on a story of the Tsar who failed to give a "halt" order to his marching troops, who marched to Siberia before being remembered and ordered back.

Charlot's *Repertoire Revue* changed programme each week for three weeks. Its leading ladies were Heather Thatcher and an 18 year old Jessie Matthews. Andre Charlot had a training school and placed a note in each programme -

During the producer's stay in Glasgow Mr Charlot will be ready to give auditions to ladies and gentlemen who consider they have talent for the stage. All those who think they are likely to make good as dancers or vocalists are invited to apply. The only condition is that each application must be accompanied by a postal order for half-a-crown, which will be handed over entirely to local hospital funds.

Jack Hylton band leader

The Alhambra housed the Jack Hylton Band's first visit to Glasgow, returning each year for 10 years, usually in summer variety, twice nightly. After the show he played at the Plaza Ballroom until 2am for gala nights. As a boy he played piano in his father's pierrot troupe visiting Girvan, and was now the most successful bandleader in Europe. The Alhambra's deputy manager Fred Ferne became his personal manager, coming back in 1937 as general manager. Hylton also became a director of the Locarno Ballroom, and a theatre impresario.

One of his singers was Ella Logan, Jimmy's aunt, before she moved to New York and international fame. In 1929, at the Alhambra, Hylton signed up pianist Billy Munn, who with his fellow Glaswegians George Chisholm and Tommy McQuater would have a major impact on jazz development in Britain.

(above)

Jack Hylton Band, Heather Thatcher, Jessie Matthews, Florence Mills

Florence Mills and the Blackbirds

In the summers of 1926 and 1927 Harlem's finest dancer, comedienne and singer, Florence Mills, now the toast of Paris, led the *Blackbirds* revue produced in Zeigfeld style, with the Plantation Jazz Orchestra, chorus and singers. The Evening Citizen enthused over:

This novel and exhilarating entertainment. Scenes include a Hotsy-Totsy Cabaret with numerous versions of the Black Bottom. Everybody dances. The Plantation Girls begin where other chorus girls leave off. The Pullman Porters and the

T
H
A
T'
S

A

G
O
O
D

G
I
R
L

Three Eddies dance on their knees as fast as others can on their feet.

She told the reporter about rhythm …"Don't bother so much about the steps. Get the beat of the music in your heart, and your feet will respond naturally. With coloured people it is as natural to Charleston as it is to breathe. We have our own people writing our music for us, and they are the most wonderful writers of jazz music in the world."

Buchanan and Broadway

Sunny, by Jack Buchanan, found it hard to stay away, with Lala *(left)* Collins as *Sunny*, and songs including Who-ooo Stole My Heart Away. The show's special train

Florence Mills, centre, in Toy Soldier parody. Scene in Sunny, Elsie Randolph & Jack Buchanan, Adele & Fred Astaire, Gracie Fields, That's a Good Girl flyer, Tallulah Bankhead

arriving at Central had 95 people, six trucks of scenery and props, one horse box for the white horse, and three dining cars. Another Buchanan success *That's a Good Girl* co-starred Elsie Randolph with Anton Dolin, the Tiller Girls and the Debroy Somers Band. The opening number was Let Yourself Go, and Fancy Our Meeting was the big hit song. Playwright Alan Melville recalls:

Jack and Elsie sang with the full chorus. They were all dressed in the palest

Alhambra Expands West

Buying property behind the theatre, and using the new share funds of the company, a major extension came into use in 1928 designed by Sir James Burnet. The wide stage, with its good spaces at the side, was doubled in depth and made flat – replacing the raked style of most theatres with its difficulties for dancers. Instead of fly ropes being manually handled by a dozen men on the first floor of the fly tower a new grid was built - of stout wood, better than steel if a fire should start - above the third floor capable of hanging 70 backcloths over the stage and for curtains and other scenery. Each cloth was hung on three wires led over wheels, with ball bearings ensuring complete silence. This system also allowed cloths and scenery to be tilted to the finest or largest degrees, and continued to be unique in Britain. The counter-weight system had 70 channels and wheels each numbered, and each with a spring buffer at the end in case a weight was dislodged – ensuring a quiet landing. All this was operated at the stage level switchboard by one man, giving speed, accuracy and economy. New lighting, switchboards and stand-by generators were introduced.

A lift was installed to all floors and a canteen added. Dressing rooms increased in number, all with showers. This would continue to be unheard of anywhere. Still unique in Britain to this day was the style of shower with water coming down from a wide neck ring at shoulder level, so that hair and makeup was unaffected. New offices were added, and a laundry. The scenery door moved into Waterloo Street and the property store moved under the enlarged stage - anything from the hind legs of an elephant to a golden throne. The stage door moved west and next to it a large theatre shop and ticket centre was created. However Hope Street won as the main box office.

Britain's last new commercial theatre was built in the same year, 1928, the Southampton Empire known today as The Mayflower.

Old methods of cleaning the theatre were ended in 1922 when an electro-turbine exhaust vacuum system, Clyde-Turbo, was installed by shipbuilders Alexander Stephens & Sons, Linthouse, using a series of fixed tubes and flexible hoses, with dust collection silos in the basement. It had tools for the cleaning of furs, dresses, clothing and stage equipment. The auditorium was vacuumed daily and the gridiron and equipment weekly, made easier by the extension's flat roof and no inaccessible places. Alhambra's grid sparkled!

(above)
A principal dressing room, a chorus dressing room, stage entrance and hall keepers office, stage and counter balance fly gear

of silver grey and the palest of silver blue. Glasgow thought it the last word in chic. So did I. There was some strange feat of levitation... their feet never seemed actually to touch the stage, or if they did, it wasn't for long. You could hardly hear a sound except for the quiet pizzicato of the strings or the occasional, very occasional, tap of Jack and Elsie's shoes.

Soon after its US premiere came *Lady Be Good*, presented by Alfred Butt, with Fred and Adele Astaire at the Alhambra for the first time. This was the Gershwin brothers' first Broadway show. *Hit the Deck* from the USA premiered at the Alhambra starring Stanley Holloway, when husky sailors first exhorted their friends to Sing Hallelujah, When Blues Pursue Ya, and More Than You Know. *The Student Prince*, promoted by Butt, opened to the music of Sigmund Romberg

The Desert Song

Opening in 1927 the successor to *Rose Marie* was *The Desert Song*, produced by Alfred Butt who found it in New York. Its composer Sigmund Romberg insisted that the orchestras should have two harps and not one, because two looked better! It opened with chorus girls dressed as French Foreign Legionnaires in a military drill dance spectacle; and Harry Welchman as the *Red Shadow*.

After a brief closure in the summer, to finalise the extension, the theatre reopened in 1928 with

(above)
Arthur Riscoe, After-theatre dancing at the Waldorf, Sauchiehall Street.
Dorthy Dickson in Tip Toes Revue

revues and variety from Sophie Tucker, Harry Lauder, Jack Buchanan and the Duncan Sisters and the first of many returns of *The Desert Song*.

Showboat

Showboat made its Glasgow debut the same year, with frequent use of spotlights - the first time in musicals. Time moved in the life of the Old Man River from the 1880s through the Chicago World Fair to 1927. Other musicals included *Funny Face*, and *The Vagabond King*, by the same hand as *Rose Marie*. *The Show's the Thing*, with Gracie Fields had a cast of 60. Comedies, revues,

Sir Alfred Butt's Time for Tea

In 1929 Sir Alfred was made a baronet. Over the next few months he retired from all his theatre directorships to concentrate on being a Conservative Member of Parliament for a London seat, which he first won in 1922.

At the Alhambra company meeting in 1930 he said: "Elaborate and extensive alterations have now been carried out in connection with the stage, and we are now in possession of one of the most modern and best equipped stages in the whole country. Consequently we will find no difficulty in presenting the most lavish and elaborate productions, not only in a scale to equal what could be done at the biggest theatre in London, but with greater economy and efficiency." He was succeeded as chairman by John Rowan, one of the co-founders.

However Sir Alfred was forced to resign from Parliament in 1936 when it was discovered he had made a fortune speculating on the future price of tea using inside knowledge of Budget plans from the then Chancellor, who also had to resign. He provided money to help Churchill wage his campaign against appeasement.

(above)

Sir Alfred and Lady Butt, racing colours

Butt focussed his interest on horse racing as owner of the Brook Stud farm in Newmarket until his passing in 1962. Of his many winners one was called Glasgow Alhambra.

plays and repertory seasons continued as did variety.

The sensuous Tallulah Bankhead, in a romantic comedy, *Her Cardboard Lover*, delighted her audience by mainly playing it in her underwear. And the same again next year. Jack House recollects Arthur Riscoe, musical comedy star of *The Girl Friend* and many more shows. Always waiting in the wings was his dresser, standing like a perfect butler with a tray on which reposed a bottle of whisky and a glass. Each time he came off the stage he had another nip just to keep him going.

(above)

Showboat at the Levee

For Christmas 1929 another Sigmund Romberg discovery by Butt packed the theatre. This was *The New Moon* about pirates bold and the French Revolution, its music including Lover Come Back to Me. Its principal, the soprano Eileen Moody, was a niece of opera's Charles Manners.

STAND
UP AND
SING

GLASGOW .
ALHAMBRA

Price - Sixpence

TOM ARNOLD, LTD., present
VIVIAN PALMER & LOUIS BARBER'S SUMMER SHOW

ALHAMBRA REVELS

FOR A SEASON COMMENCING MAY 22nd. 1939

YES SIR! THAT'S MY BABY

Words by
Gus Kahn
Music by
Walter Donaldson

DoverCards.com

Irving Berlin inc

WHO'S WONDERFUL–WHO'S MARVELOU
MISS ANNABELLE LEE

by
SIDNEY CLARE
LEW POLLACK

Irving Berlin Inc.

AIN'T SHE SWEET?

Jack Yellen
Milton Ager

AGER, YELLEN & BORNSTEIN INC.

My Blue Heaven

A FASCINATING FOX TROT BALLAD

by
WALTER DONALDSON
Words by
GEORGE WHITING

WHISPERING
JACK SMITH

WHAT IS THIS THING
CALLED LOVE?

by
COLE PORTER
FROM
CHARLES B. COCHRAN'S
LONDON REVUE
"WAKE UP AND DREAM"

HARMS

Musical Thirties, Premieres and Pantomimes

Ever Green, written in Britain by the Americans Rodgers & Hart set new standards. For its premiere in October 1930 in the Alhambra, CB Cochran built a revolving stage, the first of its type in Britain, brought over two black high-speed dance choreographers from New York, and chose Jessie Matthews as his star.

When the huge revolving stage was installed it was discovered to be too high for the first six rows of the stalls to see. Unperturbed Cochran summoned carpenters to raise the *stalls* by four feet. Rehearsals went on into the wee small hours. One of the main difficulties was that none had ever worked or danced on a revolving stage before, and as they danced in the black-out on a floor that was moving in the opposite direction to their feet, they kept smashing into each other.

Cochran addressed the opening night audience - "You are privileged tonight to see a dress rehearsal of a play... there may be hold-ups and waits, scenery may fall down..." The curtain went up late and did not come down until one-thirty. Fortunately the master showman had arranged with the Corporation to put on extra late-night trams so that they everyone got home. For each *Ever Green* show all the Alhambra programmes had a "cheque" inside by CB Cochran because the audiences were all his Extras in the show.

The song Dancing on the Ceiling was especially written by Lorenz Hart for Jessie, and it became Cochran's favourite, although the BBC banned it for a while because the word "bed" was used several times - *He dances overhead, on the ceiling, near my bed.* In the spectacle of the Fair at Neuilly 170 performers crowded onto the revolving stage with its lights, steam-organs and whirling roundabouts. In another, Jessie Matthews was bedecked in a gigantic headdress of spangle and ostrich feathers, fifteen feet high and twenty five feet wide. The following year *Hold My Hand* had its premiere, Jessie Matthews co-starring with Stanley Lupino in her

(opposite)

Dancing on the Ceiling, from Ever Green. Flyer 1930; Evelyn Laye, Jack Buchanan, Adele Dixon; Flyer 1938, Songsheets

(below)

Jessie Matthews

first musical comedy, again with the same American dance arrangers. *Sally Who?* in 1933 was her third musical premiere.

"In the Twenties and Thirties" writes Charles Oakley "the reputation of the Clydeside playgoer for discrimination has led the promoters of many of London's plays, musical comedies and revues to give their productions a "preliminary run" on Clydeside. In consequence the Glasgow visitor to London often has difficulty in finding a theatre with a presentation which he has not seen already."

(below)

Yvonne Arnaud, Bobby Howes, Richard Hearne.

Debroy Somers, Billy Mayerl, Harry Lauder postcard

Musicality

Top performers included Sophie Tucker, Harry Lauder, Jack Buchanan, Evelyn Laye, Gracie Fields, Jack Hylton & His Band, Nelson Keys, Billy Bennet, George Robey, Yvonne Arnaud, Zena Dare, Carl Brisson, the Lupino family, Harry Welchman, Arthur Riscoe, Binnie Hale, Alice Delysia, Anne Croft, Bobby Howes, Leslie Henson, Phyllis Monkman, Beatrice Lillie, Adele Dixon, Peggy O'Neil and more. New performers in comedy and musicals included Rex Harrison and Richard Hearne. The Debroy Somers Band featured in many musicals, playing on the stage. Somers previously founded the Savoy Hotel Orpheans beloved of the flappers. Billy Mayerl, lightening fingers at the piano, and who was the first in Britain to perform Gershwin's Rhapsody in Blue, co-starred in musicals with the Mayerl Band on stage. America's Eddie Mayo and His Harmonica Band toured Europe in top billing, and a ladies band headlined under the name of The 22 Ingenues, each of whom could play six or seven instruments.

Harry's back again raising a Smile

HARRY LAUDER

Audiences lapped up the return of Nikita Balieff's *Chauve-Souris*, *Folies Bergeres Revues* (twice nightly), and new editions of *The Co-optimists* while Cochran presented *Wake Up and Dream* for which Cole Porter wrote What is This Thing Called Love, and the UK premiere of *For the Love of Mike* included Got a Date With an Angel.

The Play's The Thing

Plays came from the typewriters of PG Wodehouse, including two of his premieres, JM Barrie, JB Priestley, Edgar Wallace, Noel

Coward, and Ivor Novello. Seasons of the Scottish National Players included a new actress Meg Buchanan, and the repertories of the Abbey Theatre Dublin included the works of WS Yeats, in particular *Kathleen ni Houlihan*. Sir Gerald du Maurier acted in one of his own plays, while Robert Fenemore's Masque Theatre presented AJ Cronin's *Hatter's Castle* and many more. James Bridie's *Tobias and the Angels* proved his national status. The premiere in 1932 of *Follow Me* was led by Tyrone Guthrie. Set mainly in Glasgow this was a religious play with humour, which tested the censors. The same year CB Cochran's religious play *The Miracle* ran for 3 weeks – a spectacle complete with music and a huge cast. Sir John Martin Harvey took the lead in Repertory, and in 1935 *Hamlet* spoke with the dulcet tones of John Gielgud. Plays were giving way to ballet from the mid Thirties.

Summers and Winters

Summers had fortnights of variety interchanging with revues and light musicals. Often July would be closed. Holidays down the Clyde with all the resorts' shows were real competition. In 1930, a year before her sudden death, Anna Pavlova was dancing Polish Wedding, Invitation to the Dance, and Autumn Leaves. The Festive Season's attraction continued to be a musical

(below)

Holiday Poster, Programme advert 1931, Flyer 1930, Tyrone Guthrie, James Bridie, John Gielgud

for 6-8 weeks. For 1930 this was *Stand Up and Sing* with Jack Buchanan, Ethel Stewart, Anton Dolin (before he set up his own ballet company), and Anna Neagle finding her first stardom, supported by the Debroy Somers Band. The following Christmas saw *Bitter Sweet* by Noel Coward. The tunes were enjoyed including I'll See You Again, but some of the public were indifferent, the scenes brief and the intervals long. CB Cochran promised to make amends with a new production. True to his word, Cochran came the next winter with Noel Coward's *Cavalcade* containing the last 40 years of history hammered into one musical play, and

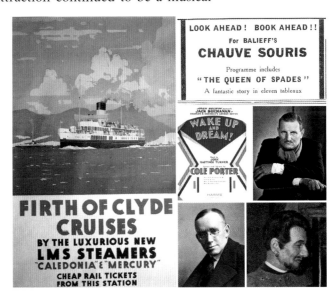

a cast of 200. The summer's attractions included a Jack Buchanan Repertory Season of three weeks, one week each of *Sunny, That's A Good Girl,* and *Stand Up and Sing,* twice daily.

Economic Slump and More Premieres

America's Stock Market crash, depression in all trades and high unemployment continued with little sign of improving. Intense competition from cinema caused anxiety. The Alhambra's profits slid steadily to zero and in 1933 it reported its first (and sizable) loss.

Ivor Novello premiered his play *Proscenium*, with himself, Fay Compton and Zena Dare, aided by a revolving stage; Andre Charlot premiered his exhilarating revue *Please* –about Napoleon and Josephine -with Beatrice Lillie and Lupino Lane (by now almost a resident of Glasgow); and James Bridie premiered his new work *A Sleeping Clergyman*, starring Robert Donat.

For Julian Wylie Productions Ltd the effervescent **Tom Arnold** stepped forward staging the musical *Casanova* with Harry Welchman and a cast of 150. He would now operate as an impresario, producing pantomimes, revues, plays, films and ice shows. 1933 also saw the play *Ballerina* open with Francis Doble, a company of 90 and Lydia Kyasht and Anton Dolin (who was appearing as an actor, rather than a dancer.)

(below)
Seating Plan, Pricing advertisment, Anna Pavlova

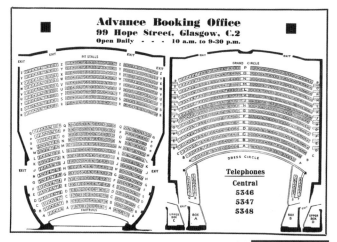

Dolin and his dancing partner Alicia Markova danced with the Vic-Wells Ballet at the Alhambra, and soon would form their own company. Just before Christmas Jack Buchanan, dry voiced and light footed, danced with Elsie Randolph in the musical *Mr Whittington* amidst frothy dresses, beautiful scenery and a Derby scene with real horses. The Festive offering was the premiere of *Jack & Jill*, a musical by Vivien Ellis and Hammerstein.

New chairman-to-be, **Douglas McInnes Shaw**, noted the Royal continued to be profitable because of the popularity of pantomimes and decided to reintroduce them to the Alhambra. It would take a few years to return to large profits.

Pantomimes Restart

In 1934 Bernard Frutin's Summertime Show was twice nightly with a change of show weekly, led by Tommy Morgan and Bert Denver. Prices were reduced for the summer month. Much heralded and under the control of Julian Wylie the Alhambra's splendidly dressed pantomime *Mother Goose* approached, led by Will Fyffe as the son of Mother Goose, George Lacy as Mother Goose, Kitty Reidy, the 16 Jackson Girls, the taller brunettes and blondes of the

Dexter Dancers and a children's chorus of 24 young girls in ballet and song. For many years Alhambra pantomime scenery was made in the studio workshops of Bill Glover, whose family had run the Theatres Royal in Dunlop Street and Hope Street.

Starting each December BBC Scotland relayed excerpts of a different pantomime each week from the city's theatres. Julian Wylie was broadcast from the Alhambra in an interview preceding the start. Asked if he was superstitious before the start of this, his 13th panto season, he cheerfully replied he was not. He died within three days of the broadcast. But the show went on as did his other five pantomimes across Britain. The Glasgow Herald reported "the fun is fast, furious and at times delicious."

In the Newspapers

Newspapers were full of the talk of war as Germany unveiled its modern rearmed Navy, Air Force and Army. Britain's national symbol of achievement and recovery, the Queen Mary, was now built and fitting out at Clydebank. Cunard commissioned Doris Zinkeisen to design the liner's Verandah Grill and night club, which she enveloped in an extensive mural on the theme of *Entertainment*. Her sister created murals for the vast Ballroom. Both also worked on the giant's sister ship Queen Elizabeth, which slid out to sea in 1940.

The country awaited a decision in 1935 about national TV while John Logie Baird's experimental service continued to run. If there was to be a BBC service it would only be for London. He said that Glasgow should have its own service using the tower the Baird Company had at the Crystal Palace which with relays could serve Glasgow and 35 miles around.

(below)

Anna Neagle and Jack Buchanan, Zena Dare, Beatrice Lillie, Robert Donat, Tom Arnold, Tommy Morgan

The Markova Dolin Company

Lew Leslie's hot-paced *Blackbirds* returned from America, while the summer season's musical offering *To Be Continued* had a change of show each week. The Vic-Wells Ballet came with Margot Fonteyn in seasons over two years. In early autumn, and having left Vic-Wells, the new Markova-Dolin Company took stage with Markova and Dolin, a Symphony Orchestra of 40, and a ballet corps in *Carnaval, Giselle, David* and other pieces. They performed until 1937 with *The Nutcracker* and other productions, choreographed by La Nijinska; and stylish costumes designed by R St John Roper. Tom Arnold presented

Alhambra
Tatler

Vol. XI.—No. 121.

Miss EUSIE RANDOLPH and Mr. JACK BUCHANAN
in a Scene from "They'll Make You Whistle."

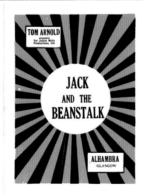

MOTHER GOOSE

ALHAMBRA
90 HOPE ST.   GLASGOW   Telephone
GLASGOW   CENTRAL 5846
Box Office   5847, 5848

Commencing WEDNESDAY, DEC. 23rd, at 6-45 p.m.
thereafter NIGHTLY at 7 p.m.   MATINEES at 2
SPECIAL MATINEES—Dec. 24th, 25th 26th, 30th, 31st; Jan. 1st, 2nd
4th, 5th, 6th, 7th, 8th and 9th at 2 p.m.

TOM ARNOLD
(For Julian Wylie Productions Ltd.) present
THE MAGNIFICENT PANTOMIME

JACK AND THE BEANSTALK
TREMENDOUS CAST INCLUDES

TOMMY MORGAN		DOROTHY WARD
SHANKS Bros.	J. Murray STEWART	Jimmie SPROLL
YVONNE KOLB	GEORGE PRENTICE	INA LAURIE
RENEE FOSTER	AND	TOMMY YORKE
NIGHTLY at 7 p.m.	G. S. MELVIN	MATINEES at 2 p.m.

C. Allen & Company, Ltd., 20, Gerrard Street, London, W.1.

TOM ARNOLD
presents
For Julian Wylie
Productions, Ltd

JACK
AND THE
BEANSTALK

ALHAMBRA
GLASGOW

Cinderella with Jay Laurier and Helen Breen, who was Arnold's wife.

There was still a scarcity of suitable attractions despite Cole Porter's *Anything Goes* produced by Cochran, and some premieres of plays and musicals including *Over She Goes* with Adele Dixon and Stanley Lupino, Teddie St Denis (native of Bearsden) and Billy Mayerl and his Band; and Lupino Lane in his musical *Twenty To One*. The Summer Show of 1936 *Good Evening Glasgow!* was accompanied by the Lou Preager Band, and failed. The theatre shut for three months. Opera fortnights made a return with the short-lived Universal Grand Opera Company. For the pantomime Tommy Morgan joined Dorothy Ward and GS Melvin in *Jack & The Beanstalk* with extra profit to the theatre, although he later returned to his usual stage at the Pavilion.

The Scout Gang Show

One innovation in 1936 became an institution, and today the Glasgow Gang show is the longest running Gang Show in the world. 150 Scouts, Rovers and Scoutmasters of the 1st Glasgow Scouts company started their annual *Gang Show*. The stage and Broadway producer Ralph Reader had responded to the London Scout Council's request for a Scout show, which saw the light in 1932. Glasgow was the second city to start a Gang Show, scripts and music by Reader, and adding Glasgow elements. Sets were made by the Glover Studios in Garscube Road. Ralph Reader was a regular visitor but the Scouts had little knowledge of production and were rescued with only a few weeks to go by the Alhambra's stage manager Jimmy Cullen, and by John Martin of Stage Furnishings in Sauchiehall Street (a stalwart of the Pantheon Club) who became the Gang's producer for many years. The annual Show went to whichever theatre was available, returning to the Alhambra in 1939, and resumed after the war.

Louis Freeman was the theatre's new music director, and his orchestra

(above)

Entertainment Murai by Doris Zinkeisen, Alicia Markova and Anton Dolin, Margot Fonteyn, Doris Zinkeisen working at Clydebank, RMS Queen Mary

(opposite)

Adverts, Crest of the Wave scenes, Jack & the Beanstalk flyer, Elsie Randolph & Jack Buchanan, Mother Goose with Will Fyffe, Lupino Lane & Teddie St Denis in Me and My Girl

became the Gang's Orchestra. His baton always had a bulb at its end, to let performers see his conducting! By a nice coincidence a few years after the Gang started Billy Corbett, grandson of the philanthropist and city dining–rooms pioneer Thomas Corbett, became Britain's Chief Scout – Lord Rowallan.

Ballets de Monte Carlo and Alhambra Revels

Both appearances in Scotland of the new Ballets de Monte Carlo took place in the Alhambra during 1937, with their orchestra of 70 players and 40 dancers under the ballet's founder M Rene Blum, brother of France's Prime Minister. The seasons included *Swan Lake*, and *Les Sylphides* based on the music of Chopin in a riot of colour and artistry. The Ministry of Labour tried to ban their visit to Britain because Britain's Vic-Wells Ballet was also on tour.

Of three musicals premiered in the year, *Me and My Girl*, set in Cockney London with Stanley Lupino and Teddie St Denis, got a cool response in Glasgow and London despite its star cast, except for some of its songs, which the BBC made famous including The Lambeth Walk, and Leaning on A Lamppost. It came back the next year to acclaim. Tom Arnold started *The Alhambra Revels* as an annual summer variety show, changing weekly, led by Alec Finlay, Scotland's Gentleman. Every Friday night was "Carnival & Gala Night – gifts for everybody."

Ice Show Supremo

Producer Tom Arnold launched his new idea – major musical ice shows – starting in 1937 with *Switzerland* which was in three parts – ice spectacle; cabaret; ice spectacle, and the following year the *Winter Sports Ice Show*. For all his ice shows for the next 30 years he chose L.Sterne & Co of Glasgow to devise the stage ice rinks,

(above)

Programme, Ballet Russes, Alec Finley, Cicely Courtneidge

refrigerating equipment and pipeworks, and make them portable after 1945, across Britain where they were maintained by Sterne's branches. L. Sterne built around 90% of all public ice rinks here, and a number overseas.

Not resting on his laurels Arnold produced even more pantomimes across the country. *Puss in Boots* saw Aberdeen's Harry Gordon thrive at the Alhambra, with Esmee Marshall as Principal Boy. The next Spring, Tom Arnold presented *Crest of the Wave* written by and starring Ivor Novello, and Dorothy Dickson. Novello now entrusted all his productions to Arnold, and the theatre manager Crossley Taylor became Novello's touring manager. W

McQueen Pope writes of the spectacular scenes in *Crest of the Wave*:

> One was a train crash, the full size Transcontinental Express dashing at speed through the night, its passengers sitting at lighted windows – and then disaster. An ear splitting explosion, a jumbled heap of flaming smoking ruins. Steel wires worked the revolving scenery and the trees and bushes hurtled by - they moved but the train did not. Another sensation was the transformation of a liner into a great battleship complete with 15 inch guns in the winking of an eye with the company singing and dancing as sailors in a number called "Nautical", very well set by Ralph Reader.

1938's Peacetime Pantomime

Annual profits returned largely thanks to *Aladdin* with Harry Gordon as Widow Twankey and supported down the bill by Alec Finlay making his pantomime debut and even playing Il Trovatore on his bagpipes. The principal dancer was Berenice Barry, sister of Markova. Magnificent palaces and pagodas appeared and vanished, and on a magic carpet Harry Gordon and Renee Foster (Aladdin) floated high over the heads of the audience – without any visible means of support. Hundreds of fairy lights illuminated the Tableaux of the Lamp on the revolving stage. The Midnight Matinee on 2nd January 1939 was in support of German Refugee Children, a fund presided over by Sir Cecil Weir, convenor of the Empire Exhibition which had attracted 13 million visitors.

Shipyards and factories were busy, civil defences and air raid shelters were being built, volunteers joined the Army, Navy and Royal Air Force reserves and still nobody knew when the war would start. Soon the city was full of servicemen and women. By the end of 1939 Harry Gordon, always the best-dressed pantomime Dame, declared he was "the best looking hen in the Wrens."

New Records

Early in the fateful year of 1939 Jessie Matthews and Sonnie Hale brought their new musical *I Can Take It* to the Alhambra for five weeks. As before, her numbers and exquisite dance ensembles were by her New York production team. Her dancing partner was Hal Thompson, who

(above)

Aladdin revolving stage, Louise Rainer, Empire Exhibition 1938, I Can Take It flyer 1939, Midnight Matinee, Jessie Matthews being sketched by Copland & Lye's store artist Roy

had partnered Ginger Rogers. 18,000 people saw it in the first week, and the next week Jessie Matthews broke the theatre's attendance record held by Jack Buchanan, and the third week exceeded the second. It toured extensively but could not open in London because of the approach of war. *The Fleet's Lit Up* with Stanley Lupino was "vivacious entertainment for the broad-minded and a riot of fun. A bright show for dark days."

Five thousand fans crowded the Central Station to greet the German-born film star Luise Rainer, the first actress to win an Oscar back to back, coming for her British debut in a comedy play *Behold the Bride*. On Sunday she read the lessons at Trinity Church at a service for the Refugee Fund, jointly led by the minister and by the rabbi of Garnethill Synagogue. The summer's *Alhambra Revels* included a snake dancer as near to the nude as anything in the Folies Bergère. This was the Dawnya and Petrov Snake Dance from Paris, who changed their dance each week. Ships of the French Navy were in town and, on seeing a flyer in French, the Admiral instructed the ships' companies to march in uniform from the docks to the theatre. Jean Adrienne sang in French for the sailors, and the Admiral sent a letter of thanks.

Col. Douglas McInnes Shaw | Alhambra Chairman

Douglas McInnes Shaw, the son of former Lord Provost Sir Archibald McInnes Shaw, was a director in the family firm of Shaw & McInnes, Maryhill Ironworks, pipe and architectural ironfounders, and a grandson of the last Provost of Maryhill. During the Great War he was decorated for bravery for the capture of over 100 Germans (in-

cluding Prince Hohenlohe) and became the youngest Battalion Commander in the British Army at age 23. He served again in the next World War.

He was elected to Glasgow Corporation, and in 1924 became Member of Parliament for West Renfrewshire. From 1924 to 1946 he was Grand Master of the Orange Lodge of Scotland and in his last three years of office was also elected Imperial Grand President of Great Britain and the Dominions.

(above)
Col. Douglas McInnes Shaw, Iron Moulders

He and his wife Dorothy, a keen golfer, moved to Symington, Ayrshire, whose station did not have stopping trains late in the evenings. However after the Alhambra shows he would often walk up the platform at St Enoch's and have a chat with the engine driver for the Ayr train. To the surprise of other passengers there was an un-scheduled stop at Symington! He became Convenor of Ayrshire County Council and was knighted for public and political services in 1953.

Sir Harry Lauder

After giving up his job as a coal miner in Hamilton and touring the halls in Scotland as comedian and minstrel, Harry Lauder gained national notice in 1900 with his Irish comic song Calligan, Call Again. A fine actor, he created a series of character studies in comedy and pathos, interspersed with a spot of piano playing and baritone singing, honed to perfection. He emerged on stage "like the sun from base clouds."

By far Britain's best known entertainer for 40 years, Harry Lauder was the first British artiste to sell one million records. During WWI Lauder's concerts and world tours raised £1m for the Harry Lauder Fund "to establish in new and suitable occupations the maimed and blinded soldiers and sailors of Scotland." On going to France he was the first British artiste to insist on singing in the trenches and not just at hospitals and base camps. He was knighted in 1919.

Sir Harry Lauder packed theatres and concert halls on every continent including 22 tours across America, travelling in his own "Harry Lauder Special" train. His American agent insisted always on him wearing the kilt, which became part of his trademark. He had seven world tours. During WWII his concert party travelled throughout Britain entertaining at all the service bases - his party being himself, pianist Harry Carmichael, solo violinist Zus Wiseman, and singer Kathy Kaye. Winston Churchill's favourite song was Keep Right on to the End of the Road, and when he addressed America and Canada in person in the dark days of 1940 he quoted lines from Lauder.

(above)
Sir Harry Lauder rehearsal at the Alhambra

Evelyn Lane

International star of stage and film, comic actress, dancer and singer, Evelyn Laye possibly had the longest career of any leading ladies. Her signature tune was I'll See You Again closely followed by Lover Come Back To Me. Her first of many Alhambra shows was in 1916, age 16, in a revue Honi Soit by Robert Courtneidge, the first producer to pay chorus members for rehearsals, and to provide casts with paid holidays. This was her first year on stage, and Scottish newspapers gave her her first review. In the Alhambra pantomime starting in 1940, she was paid £2,000 a week, much more than her next in line Harry Gordon. Her last time at the Alhambra was in the musical Strike A Light in 1966.

Her first love was a submariner who died in WW1. In Glasgow in a Cochran premiere Lights Up, in 1939, at the civic lunch in the City Chambers she was asked by a friend Lord Inverclyde, chairman of Cunard, if she would sing at a British Sailors Society charity concert in the Empire Theatre. He was the Society's Chairman. She agreed on the understanding he would ask the Admiralty to let her provide a concert for the sailors at Britain's largest Naval base Scapa Flow, set in its bleakest northern location and seemingly forgotten. Eventually, and after the King intervened,

(above)
Evelyn Lane

the Admiralty finally said yes. She staged very welcome concerts there, and raised money in numerous theatres for her Scapa Flow Fund. The following year 1940 the government started ENSA to provide entertainment for all the armed forces, and she was put in command of entertainments for the Senior Service.

In London in the 1920s on stage in a musical Evelyn Laye totally lost her voice but successfully consulted Lionel Logue of Harley Street. She advised an ardent admirer from his bachelor days, who would remain infatuated by her, to do the same, to help cure his stammer – Albert, Duke of York, the future King George VI. The actress, therapist, king and queen remained friends, and in 1994 Queen Elizabeth, the Queen Mother, wrote to Downing Street requesting a Damehood to be awarded to Evelyn, but Prime Minister John Major declined.

Jack Buchanan

On leaving Glasgow Academy, Jack Buchanan tholed office work only by appearing in the newly formed Glasgow Amateur Operatic Society. His professional debut in variety was in the Panopticon, Trongate and in a play in the Grand, Cowcaddens, returning always to the Society's shows and then moving to London. He became Britain's top show dancer, acting in revues, musicals, comedies and plays for theatre and film, feted on both sides of the Atlantic. Styling himself on Eugene Stratton, of Lily of Laguna fame who finished his songs with a soft-shoe dance, he soon developed with his leading ladies an appealing and languid sort of tap dance. He appeared in the Alhambra frequently from 1914, starting in fourth billing, and a few years later in top billing.

The London Times described "the seemingly lazy but most accomplished grace with which he sang, danced, flirted and joked his way through musical shows. The tall figure, the elegant gestures, the friendly drawling voice, the general air of having a good time." The debonair entertainer set fashion, Eddie Ashton recalling "the local boy whose charm lit up the theatre like a searchlight and whose clothes were the envy and example of every young man about Renfield Street." In evening wear he made white tie and tails popular because of his shows.

He presented shows and plays, and owned theatres and film studios. He often premiered his shows in the Alhambra and promoted new entertainers. For many years the back of the London Telephone Directories had only two words JACK BUCHANAN. He helped many financially and in wartime ensured shows continued to give employment and entertainment. From their schoolboy days in Helensburgh he helped fund and support John Logie Baird's pioneering of television and was chairman of the Baird Company which also devised, produced and rented television sets.

Jack Buchanan's signature songs include And Her Mother Came Too, I'm In A Dancing Mood, Fancy Our Meeting, Good-Night Vienna, and Who...? His last show in the Alhambra was in 1952 in King's Rhapsody, penned by Ivor Novello.

(above)
Jack Buchanan

Jessie Matthews

Becoming Britain's international film goddess in the 1930s Jessie Matthews had already triumphed in theatre musicals after serving her apprenticeship in revues in the 1920s. As a child she had more natural ability in dance than Alice Marks (Markova) who attended the same ballet classes. By 1926 she was head-lining shows by CB Cochran and Charlot's Revues in Britain and America.

In leading the 1930 premiere of the musical Ever Green at the Alhambra. No, No, Nanette had found its match. For the next decade or so most of her musicals opened in the Alhambra, whose stage she was delighted to find was flat – "at other theatres the stage is raked so steeply I feel I am dancing into the orchestra pit." She used her New York team in all her shows and films; the choreographer Buddy Bradley (whose clients included Fed Astaire, Ginger Rogers and Jack Buchanan) was now established in London, arranging all dance ensembles and big numbers, usually about 12, with Jessie in most; music and playwriting was also by New Yorkers.

Her films for Gaumont who now also owned Moss Empires out-sold any others. In America she was known as The Dancing Divinity. In 1938 in the World's Best Legs competition Jessie Matthews and Marlene Dietrich tied for first place. Ginger Rogers came second. After 1945 few major musicals were being made but she remained in variety and plays, on stage and radio, including Mrs Dale's Diary. Her songs include Over My Shoulder, A Room with a View, Got to Dance My Way to Heaven, In the Gloaming by the Fireside, and Everything's in Rhythm with My Heart.

(above)
Jessie Matthews

Ivor Novello

Composer, author of revues, and silent film star with a following similar to Rudolph Valentino, Ivor Novello developed as the master of grand musicals and lush melodies often in romantic drama and pageant. He was a regular at the Alhambra, acting and directing. In 1937 Crossley Taylor, the Alhambra's general manager, became Novello's touring manager.

In 1914 Novello's song Keep the Home Fires Burning (Till the Boys Come Home) became a favourite of the war, and later in the 1940's his song We'll Gather Lilacs expressed the same sentiments. Out of revues and his musicals such as *Glamorous Night, Careless Rapture, The Dancing Years, Perchance to Dream* and *King's Rhapsody* come the melodies of I Can Give You the Starlight, My Dearest Dear, Someday My Heart Will Awake, and Love is My Reason.

(above)
Ivor Novello

THE ALHAMBRA TATLER
CHRISTMAS AND NEW YEAR NUMBER. 1939-1940

REDUCED
PRICES
TO
MEMBERS
OF H. M.
FORCES

No better Gift

Send him your photograph by
SCOTTISH STUDIOS LTD
196 CLYDE STREET, GLASGOW, C.1.
50 YARDS EAST OF SUSPENSION BRIDGE
'Phone Dorothy Nelson Central 6472-3

ALHAMBRA

Commencing Saturday, 21st Dec. at 6.30 p.m.
Thereafter Nightly at 6.45 p.m.
MATINEES (as hereunder) at 2 p.m.

TOM ARNOLD presents

EVELYN LAYE

THE SLEEPING BEAUTY

ALEC FINLAY   MARJORIE BROWNE
HILDA MEACHAM   JACK HOLDEN
FELICITY ANDREAE   ELLIS CARLYLE   GORDON WHELAN

HARRY GORDON

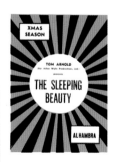

XMAS
SEASON

TOM ARNOLD
(for Julian Wylie Productions, Ltd.)
presents

THE SLEEPING
BEAUTY

ALHAMBRA

Accordingly, We Are At War..

A fortnight after war was declared on 3rd September 1939 theatres and cinemas re-opened. After a few months Tom Honeyman, the city's director of art, organised **Garrison Evenings** on Sunday evenings and sometimes a whole week. These were for the armed services, providing variety entertainment and classical entertainment in venues such as the King's, Athenaeum, Alhambra, Paramount and Lyric. Civilians could only gain entry if they were in the company of servicemen or women.

Charles Macdona started a season of the Macdona Players, in Scotland after a gap of ten years – performing George Bernard Shaw plays including the six hour version of *Man and Superman*. Shaw revived *Geneva*, his riposte to dictators. Music for the season was played by Louis Freeman and George Bowie. New plays included Bridie's *What Say They*, led by Yvonne Arnaud. Its programme intimated:

> The theatre will relay the Broadcast Message by Her Majesty the Queen to the Women of the Empire, arranged for Saturday 11th November at 9pm.

Vic-Wells Ballet with Margot Fonteyn staged eight ballets. Because of the shortage of men two pianos took the place of an orchestra. Their choreographer Frederick Ashton said going on tour improved the company's dancing and created incentives – instead of being in London when audiences could be taken for granted. *The White Horse Inn* was a cure for black-out blues. A new arrival was *The Women*, presented in Britain and America by Jack Buchanan, with an all woman cast of 40, and written by American suffragist and future ambassador Clare Boothe. Another was the Wilson Barrett-Esmond Knight Repertory Company with a comedy play. Wilson Barrett was not yet to know that his main base of patrons would be the Alhambra for 14 years.

(above)

Muriel Barron

(opposite)

Harry Gordon and cartoon as Buttons, Sleeping Beauty flyer 1940, Programme adverts, View of theatre from bus station.

Cinderella and the Enchanted Lake

For the 1939/40 pantomime *Cinderella* Tom Arnold tried to secure Stan Laurel to lead it, supported by Harry Gordon. At the same time Will Fyffe who was top of his profession throughout Britain and popular in films here and abroad (making some 23) was being sought out to do more films in Hollywood by Glasgow-born producer Frank Lloyd, a founder and past president of the Academy of Motion Picture Arts and Sciences. He flew an emissary to London to sign a new deal but Will Fyffe said he wanted to stay and do his bit for Britain.

From 1941 Fyffe and Gordon would create a new partnership in pantomime. Harry Gordon was Buttons and Muriel Barron was Prince Charming.

Born in Glasgow, she joined D'Oyly Carte Opera – moving on to become a leading lady in major musicals and a favourite singer in Ivor Novello's.

Currie's Waterfalls were spectacular with changing colour lights, similar to the Empire Exhibition, and Tyrwhitt Drake's Miniature Ponies and magnificent Crystal Coach provided the transport.

The junior chorus were the 16 Alhambra Babes. All the youngsters had to be out the theatre by 9.30pm. Timing was everything. So was swimming. In one Act there was a marble pool occupying almost the whole of the stage, beyond and surrounding it a mystic garden. The Prince appealed to the Fairy Godmother to help him find the missing slipper. She summons her Water Nymphs and bids them go into the Enchanted Lake to search. The fairies, wearing chiffon dresses looking like seaweed, walk into the water, down, down into the blue depths. Beautiful girl after beautiful girl disappears and none reappears, except one - the last Babe finds the slipper! Under the water the others swam through a chamber below the stage to dry land.

(above)
Pantomime 1939, wartime programe, Wilson Barrett

Wilson Barrett adds to Alhambra's Menu

Chairman McInnes Shaw reported the year's profits would have been higher but for some shows cancelling due to the outbreak of war including Covent Garden English Opera - who announced their seasons would be at the Alhambra because of its stage facilities, instead of the Theatre Royal. Also *No, No, Nanette* cancelled, with newsvendors declaring NO, NO, NOT YET. The new Barrett repertory acting company had stuck its toe in the water in 1939 in London, and Edinburgh's Empire, followed by an equally poorly attended national tour. Wilson Barrett writes:

> However, Glasgow made up for it. It was the first time we had ever played at the Alhambra and when we opened there on the Monday night to a full house and a wonderful welcome to us all, we knew we were home again. During that

week at the Alhambra the future of the company was settled, although we did not appreciate then to what extent. Fred Ferne, the General Manager of the Alhambra, asked us to come back the following year for a twelve-week season in the summer, and we accepted. If it had not been for this I do not think, looking back, that we could possibly have survived what was ahead of us.

For the next 14 years Alhambra's entertainment calendar would be the very best of pantomimes for almost five months each winter, three months each summer of the Wilson Barrett company producing plays and the other months major musicals usually 2-3 weeks each (and sometimes 6 weeks), ice-shows usually 4-6 weeks, ballet and other plays. Soon into the war *No, No, Nanette*

did come back, again and again - as did *Showboat, The Student Prince, Chu Chin Chow, Rose Marie*; and *The Vagabond King* with Webster Booth and Anne Zeigler.

More Musicals

In 1940 Ivor Novello, brought his latest show *The Dancing Years*, co-starring Muriel Barron and choreographed by Freddie Carpenter. Jack Buchanan premiered his musical *Top Hat and Tails*, co-starring Elsie Randolph and Fred Emny. Buchanan presented plays, and started a touring pantomime with many of his co-stars from musicals. Bobby Howes and Binnie Hale

led a revival of *Mr Cinders*, based on Cinderella, with its hit tune Spread A little Happiness. In Cole Porter's first wartime hit *Let's Face It*, Howes was joined by newcomer Pat Kirkwood. Cole Porter's music was everywhere including the season of *Du Barry Was A Lady,* and in 1943 the Alhambra staged the British premiere of his *Panama Hattie* with Bebe Daniels, Richard Hearne and Max Wall. Onstage in musicals were the bands of Caroll Gibbons and of Billy Mayerl, and headlining in variety George Elrick's Band, on a break from Green's Playhouse ballroom.

New revues opened with Hermione Gingold, Elisabeth Welch, and musical comedies with Cicely Courtneidge and Jack Hulbert. Oscar Strauss's operettas struck a chord including *A Waltz Dream. The Chocolate Soldier* especially was a favourite. So too, Richard Tauber singing in *The Land of Smiles* with

(above)

The Dancing Years, newspaper advert 1943, Fred Emny, Pat Kirkwood, Bebe Daniels

its signature melody You Are My Heart's Delight; and he returned often in *Blossom Time*, and *Old Chelsea*. International Music Weeks were held in venues including the Alhambra, with classical performances by the new Anglo Polish Ballet, Glasgow Orpheus Choir conducted by (Sir) Hugh Roberton, the Polish Army Choir and Glasgow's international pianist Frederic Lamond.

(above)
Hermione Gingold,
Cicely Courtneidge
& Jack Hulbert,
Elisabeth Welch,
Richard Tauber,
Hugh S Roberton,
Diana Churchill,
Tamara Desni

After Germany invaded the Soviet Union performances took place of Russian Opera and dance.

Dramas and Comedies

Plays by Bridie, GB Shaw and Somerset Maugham were joined by others with war-time themes including *Lifeline*, an epic about the Merchant Navy, and a comedy play *Other People's Houses* claimed to be the first to deal with Evacuees, Food Rationing, Servant Shortages, ARP and other wartime problems.

Well into their stride the **Wilson Barrett Company** staged 15-20 plays each summer. Established and new plays were presented. In weekly repertory, rehearsals for the next week's play took place during the day, while the current week's was played in the evenings. Season tickets started in 1942, individually and for families, ensuring the same seats each week. Costume supplies had come from London but proved erratic. In 1943, as Barrett writes:

The increasing prosperity of the Glasgow season made me more than ever determined to build up our own wardrobe. We bought every scrap of unrationed stuff, sets of curtains, table-cloths, bedspreads everything. The press wrote of our difficulties and we were overwhelmed with offers of items stored away in trunks and boxes, dresses that went back well over a hundred years – original silks, satins, velvets and brocades.

After a few years a warehouse was purchased in Edinburgh for props, and costumes numbering around 3,000. Under Isabel Imrie music at the Alhambra was supplied by two pianists – including herself, Jean Milligan, Arthur Blake and Eric Stapleton. Shakespeare plays broke box office records in Glasgow, but not in Edinburgh's Lyceum where they were told to bring no more! *Henry V* had the largest cast at the Alhambra – 80 in all, comprising the entire double company, extras from London, members of Rutherglen Repertory Company, and soldiers from Maryhill Barracks.

Mona Inglesby and the International Ballet

Starting with modest resources the International Ballet became the first British dance company to tour continental Europe, and opened the new Royal Festival Hall in London in 1951. As well as being a young leading dancer Mona Inglesby was a choreographer who restaged authentic versions of the large Russian classics and created new ballets. Her chief producer and mentor was Nicolai Serguéeff, the last head of the Imperial Ballet of St Petersburg. He rescued for posterity the dance notations of

that Ballet and instilled in the new company that one of the great strengths of the Imperial company was the superb quality of mime.

She had danced with continental companies and studied with the Maryinsky ballerinas in Paris, émigrés from Russia, of whom she recalls "the ballerinas moved with a femininity I had never seen in Britain." When the war started she volunteered as an ambulance driver. She writes in her memoirs:

> "The International Ballet was our desire to try and save the classical ballets from complete disappearance because, owing to the war, dancers had disbanded almost everywhere. I knew that unless some action was taken to continue the ballet profession in this country, it would take years to build up again simply because a dancer's training takes about eight years before attaining a high standard of proficiency. A whole generation of dancers could have been lost as a result of World War II, and I considered it our contribution to the war effort to help keep theatre open, allowing a population starved of relaxation and entertainment to have an opportunity to savour classical ballet of a high standard throughout blacked-out Britain."

(above)

Souvenir brochure, Mona Inglesby, Giselle by the International Ballet

Because of their large audiences they generated a substantial income which supported their innovations and overseas tours. For its 12 years it paid its way without public funding. However, by 1953 television broadcasting restarted and was affecting audiences, and the Arts Council began giving public subsidy to Sadler's Wells and Ballet Rambert but refused International Ballet's modest application. Mona Inglesby retired the company.

Ballet for the People

One of the new companies from 1939 was Lydia Kyasht's touring Ballet de la Jeunesse Anglaise. Refugees who had danced with the Warsaw Ballet started the large Anglo Polish Ballet in 1940, with more joining as they managed to escape, performing its Polish and international repertoire often at the Alhambra. They became the first ballet company to entertain troops overseas.

Above all, classical ballet was made popular by 22 year old ballerina **Mona Inglesby** who premiered her company **The International Ballet** on 19th May

1941 in the Alhambra. She opened with 21 dancers, including 15 year old Moira Shearer making her debut, and a full orchestra. One of her main designers was Doris Zinkeisen. It grew to be a very large company, bringing ballet to the masses in city theatres, cinemas, seaside holiday camps and military camps across Britain. Her company attracted top designers, composers, musicians and dancers from many countries. They had colourful and adventurous costumes; created new audiences; and started lectures in schools explaining ballet. One of many new ballets was her glamorous production of *Twelfth Night*, the first two-act ballet created for a British company, which added the novelties of song in the Greig score and dramatic voice of a Shakespearean actor.

(above)
Harry Gordon &
Will Fyffe examine
Jack's magic beans,
Vanessa Lee, Leslie
Henson
(opposite)
Bless the Bride
finale
The Scout Gang
Show
Alec Finlay, Duncan
Macrae, Robert
Wilson and Harry
Gordon in Aladdin
Gay's the Word,
with Cicely
Courtneidge
Alhambra Posters

Pantomime Partnerships

Following the elegant footsteps of Evelyn Laye, Will Fyffe, as Idle Jack in *Dick Whittington* took pole position, partnering Harry Gordon for the next six years. Gordon wove in songs and sketches as the Laird o'Inversnecky, his fictitious village, helped by the youngsters in the audience as the Inversnecky Bairns. To the happy mixture were added the Dagenham Girl Pipers.

At the war's end Arnold restarted his six-week seasons of spectacular skating and cabaret shows on ice, starting with the glamorous *Hot Ice*. This was his first national touring show, with casts headed by Olympic and World skating champions from Canada and America.

Entertainment a la Carte

In the new peacetime food remained rationed but the Alhambra's menu was in full supply. New musicals included *Bob's Your Uncle* led by Leslie Henson (with the orchestra under Mantovani), *Serenade* with America's Irene Manning, *Caprice* with Sally Ann Howes making her stage debut, Ivor Novello's *Perchance To Dream*, and *Kings Rhapsody* featuring Vanessa Lee. And in 1949 *Waltzes from Vienna* was premiered with leading lady Fay Lenore and a cast of 90 including a Viennese choir of 32. The Evening Times reported:

cout Souvenir Booklet
PRICE 9d.

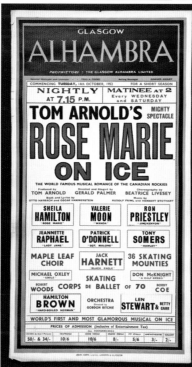

It is a relief to luxuriate in the Straussian world – a world of joyous rhythm unwedded to art values except those of the senses.

The Anglo Polish Ballet returned, as did The International Ballet. In the summers Wilson Barrett plays packed the house. Tom Arnold Ice Shows did the same each winter just before the annual pantomimes. One era ending was CB Cochran's. His last major musical *Bless the Bride*, directed by Wendy Toye, proved highly successful, with hit tunes such as La Belle Marguerite, and Lovely Day. Another was Ivor Novello's. A year later in 1950 he staged his last new work, but without him acting, in the fast moving musical *Gay's The Word* with Cicely Courtneidge playing the part of Gay.

Pantomime Moves
Alec Finlay moved to top billing in *Humpty Dumpty* with Harry Gordon. The Glasgow Herald wrote of *Puss in Boots* the following year:

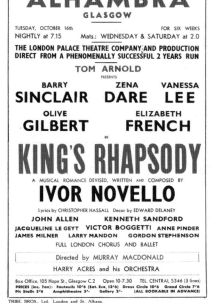

It is lavishly staged and dressed, presenting in these drab days a feast of colour to please the eye and warm the heart. Of many fine scenes Catland stands out, with a ballet in which various breeds of "cats" take part. Alec Finlay is ideally cast in the role of Simple Simon, and his musical act with clarinet is a brilliant piece of quiet fooling. As a statue of William Wallace having a chat with Mary Queen of Scots (Harry Gordon), a singing auctioneer, or when singing "Glasgow on the Clyde" in which he argues with an Edinburgh man, he provides excellent comedy. Harry Gordon as the Queen wears a large number of Dame costumes. Each year these become less extravagant and more beautifully tailored. He has two very good characteristic numbers – "Tessie the Tonic of the Trossachs" and "Steamie Jeannie."

(above)

Irene Manning, Sally Ann Howes, Sir Douglas McInnes Shaw, Babes in the Wood 1946, King's Rhapsody 1951, Programme Cover

Tom Arnold ensured clowns were in his pantomimes and ice shows. *Humpty Dumpty* had the Cairoli Brothers and *Dick Whittington* in 1949 had the musical clowns the Rastellis who could each play almost every instrument in the orchestra. They were famed for knocking each other's heads off, smashing guitars over themselves, and blowing up a piano which one of them had been playing only seconds before. When the Government was nationalising Britain's main industries, the Glasgow Herald's leader at Christmas was about PANTOMIME:

They have changed remarkably little in a changing world. Pantomime is essentially the sort of entertainment which ought not to be hurried. Every scene from opening chorus on the village green to grand finale in the palace must be taken slowly and spaciously enough to permit its personalities to be identified, plots to be disentangled.

(below)

Natalie Krassovska, Festival Ballet 1950, Beau Danube

Moreover, there is no more satisfactory feeling than one's knowledge, when the interval comes and the lights go up and the ice creams appear, that there is still a good hour and a half of magic, beauty and wit to go. They must have time enough to persuade us that they are the real world, and the dark streets into which we eventually emerge only a dream.

The Alhambra company bought 105 Hope Street in 1949 for a new Box Office, in place of the leased premises at 99, and completed theatre renewal work delayed by the war. The chairman was especially proud of the Alhambra having the longest bar in Scotland! A powerful Lamp Room was added above the Gallery Bar roof - between the two towers - for a main spotlight to the stage, 12 spotlights inserted in the

Gallery front, and six spotlights in the Circle front. Chairman McInnes Shaw reported that "the Company has now one of the most completely and excellently equipped theatres in the country."

Festival Ballet

Alicia Markova and Anton Dolin had gone their own ways in 1937, but after many years mainly in America they renewed their dancing partnership, creating their Festival Ballet company at the end of 1949, ahead of the Festival of Britain. They shared the same ideals as the pioneering Mona Inglesby, to take popular ballet to the widest geographical audiences at a price they could afford. After opening at Newcastle they came next to the Alhambra, the company returning annually (and much later renaming itself as the English National Ballet.) Festival Ballet ran large ballets and when required used supernumeraries from the Glasgow dance schools, notably the Lillian McNeil Dance School, to dress the stage for crowd scenes and the opening of carriage doors.

Unfortunately Markova damaged her ankle during a rehearsal in the theatre in October 1951, but insisted on continuing with *The Nutcracker*. Her famed dancing career now came to an end, except for an occasional guest appearance, but she continued directing. Off stage Dolin and Markova had no time for each other. After each performance the principals would go off to the Malmaison at the Central for a meal, Dolin selecting his own table where he held court, and Markova then entering and choosing a distant table with her entourage. One principal was the American, Natalie Krassovska (a Russianised name, as usual) who was known also as Natalie Leslie because of her Scottish ancestry. Scintillating on stage, she was a known scatterbrain, and could never remember what name to use when signing cheques. To ensure she got to the Malmaison each evening one of the supernumeraries was detailed to escort her from the stage door the 50 yards in a straight line to the Malmaison. Left to her own she would go off North, South or West.

Mona Inglesby's International Ballet last productions in the Alhambra were in 1952, with *The Sleeping Princess*, *Coppelia*, *Swan Lake* and other full

The Wilson Barrett Company

After the 1941 summer season of repertory plays in the Alhambra, Edinburgh became a second Barrett city following an invitation to perform at its Royal Lyceum theatre. Barrett opened his office nearby. And Aberdeen also became a Barrett city after a trial season at His Majesty's in 1947. Two companies of artistes were now engaged. Glasgow was over a full Summer, Edinburgh and Aberdeen alternating between Spring and Autumn. In his memoirs Bill Barrett describes his experiences:

"**A Repertory Theatre** is a place where, apart from a few youngsters of definite ability who are learning their job the hard way, only the most experienced actors should be engaged. I have worked in theatre for over thirty years, and I have founded and run for fourteen years a company, which, to put it at its lowest, is financially the most successful in the British Isles…………there is far more first-class acting to be seen in a tour of the established Repertory Theatres of Great Britain than you will ever see in a London season.

We have opened each year with a big overdraft at the bank (in today's money £120,000.) We reduce this through the year, thanks to the huge capacity of the Glasgow Alhambra, plus the enthusiasm of Glasgow audiences, but when we return to the smaller capacity of the Edinburgh Lyceum, the deficit creeps up again slowly but surely, and during our Christmas break, when all the staffs in our big workshops are getting ready for the coming year, making new scenery, costumes, productions, and repairs, all with no revenue coming in, it soars up.

If a first-class standard of production in Repertory is to be kept up, then every penny coming in must be used. Yet we are allowed no tax relief of any kind. A play supported by the Arts Council can play tax free in London but we have to pay full entertainment tax on everything we produce, because we are "commercial". We are given no subsidies, we are helped in no way by the Arts Council or any other body.

(above)

Wilson Barrett, 1950 flyer, Lennox Milne, Walter Carr, John Cairney, Edith McArthur

What is it that these (Arts Council) people want? Their golden rule seems to be that never should a play be produced that is likely to appeal to any but an extremely limited number of people who pride themselves on being considerably more cultured and intelligent than the rest of us - and if by chance such a play does become a popular success then obviously it must be bad. Our plays from Shakespeare to Shaw have every ingredient of greatness in them, .and because they are written by master craftsmen they have an appeal to every section of the theatre-going public."

The Wilson Barrett Company presented around 450 plays across Scotland.

length classical ballets now becoming the vogue. Also staged was *Sea Legend*, the first ballet from Australia presented by an overseas company. A few years earlier she declined the offer to be Moira Shearer's rival ballerina in the famed film, *The Red Shoes*, wary of Michael Powell's direction. Later she wistfully regretted her decision.

The Wilson Barrett Company

Wilson Barrett seasons presented plays from Shakespeare to Shaw, Rattigan to Ibsen, Sheridan to Goldsmith and others emerging as playwrights. They were the first in Glasgow to stage Arthur Miller's new play *Death of a Salesman*.

(below)

Wilson Barrett Company Van, Jack Anthony, Robert Wilson, Jeanette Raphael, Duncan Macrae, Harry Gordon, Alec Finlay

As a contribution to the Festival of Britain they put on a special series of the plays of James Bridie. There was a permanent company of around 25 and guest artistes of around 45 in any one year. Guest producers were invited in addition to company producers who included, Richard Matthews, Joan Kemp-Welch and CB Pulman.

In 1952 the Company was invited to tour South Africa with eight plays. They sailed out in the *Arundel Castle* in blazing sunshine and found themselves "back in a pre-war world, with eight-course dinners, double whiskies at one-and-three and cigarettes at half-a-crown for fifty." During the voyage they rehearsed for two hours each morning in the dining room, and were asked to take over the ship's concert. Landing in Cape Town they opened a few days later....... "to the usual glittering Johannesburg first night, all mink and diamonds."

Alhambra Team of Comic Experts

Alhambra's pantomimes were joined from 1950 by Duncan Macrae and tenor Robert Wilson – The Voice of Scotland – whose recordings include Down in the Glen, A Gordon for Me, Misty Island, and I Dream of Jeannie. When reviewing *Babes in the Wood* in 1953 the Glasgow Herald described the "Alhambra Team of Comic Experts" with Jack Anthony (in place of Harry Gordon) joining Alec Finlay and Duncan Macrae:

Each member's own particular talents – the small-boy friendliness of Finlay, Anthony's effervescent optimism, Macrae's outraged dignity – are set on display singly and jointly. Indeed this pantomime might well serve as a shortened course of study of the Glasgow school of comedy in action. Duncan Macrae's solo as an Ice Queen – the "Queen of Crossmyloof" - yearning for the affections of "Flash McGinty, halfback of the Polmadie Panthers" is possibly the most successful spot in the show but the others, Finlay's bespectacled goalkeeper and Anthony's poet are not far behind.

With so much fun being made it is not surprising if the story is sometimes lost sight of. The bones, however, are there. The bad baron seeks to dispose of the Babes and hires the robbers to do so. The children are duly abandoned in Nottingham Forest and found by Robin Hood and his merry men. Scenically the pantomime is well up to the Alhambra standard with an especially attractive Toyland scene, and a flying ballet, when the forest birds look after the Babes.

This was Tom Arnold's 17th pantomime at the Alhambra and the last one of Glasgow Alhambra Ltd. In many of these Harry Gordon was the Dame. To me, said Alec Finlay, Harry Gordon was always "Maggie." "We played seven seasons together, and Maggie was always the favourite name of Harry's Dame character. Sometimes he was my mother, sometimes my sweetheart. And sometimes we'd forget which, but we always knew we were closely related."

Howard & Wyndham Ltd buys the Alhambra

Howard & Wyndham helped Canadian Roy Thomson's plans for commercial television, agreeing to sell him the Theatre Royal (their most profitable theatre, but now showing its age) and to supply artistes for his planned Scottish Television service. Before this could happen they needed a new flagship theatre. The candidate was obvious, there was nothing to match the Alhambra. Also, it had a continuing alliance with Moss Empires, chaired by Prince Littler who chaired many theatre combines including Howard & Wyndham.

(above)
Touring poster

An offer to buy Glasgow Alhambra Ltd was accepted in 1953 – with substantial gain to the many shareholders. Sadly, during negotiations in Manchester the Alhambra's general manager, Fred Ferne, collapsed and died. From 1954, until the Royal changed to being the Scottish Television Theatre three years later, *Half Past Eight* (becoming *Five Past Eight*) and some other shows moved down Hope Street to Waterloo Street, with both theatres staging separate Howard & Wyndham pantomimes, promoting Jimmy Logan and Stanley Baxter.

A casualty was the Wilson Barrett Company whose 1954 season was moved up the hill to the Royal. Their 10,000 a week audience, many of them season ticket holders, was loyal to the Alhambra, and television was starting to have an effect. Bill Barrett closed the company at the end of the year.

Wilson Barrett Productions

(top left)

George & Margaret
- Pat Sandys and
Richard Matthews

(top right)

The School for
Scandal - Elaine
Wells and Norman
Scace

(centre left)

The Taming of the
Shrew - Richard
Matthews and Anne
Brook

(centre right)

Julius Caesar -
Derek Walker

(bottom)

Dangerous Corner
- Carol Tennant and
Robert James

Accordingly, We Are At War..

Pantomime seasons starting in 1917, after touring pantomimes in 1912-1916		
1917	*Dick Whittington*	Harry Weldon, Ella Retford
1918	*Jack and the Beanstalk*	Dorothy Ward, Shaun Glenville, Annie Croft
1919	*Cinderella*	Harry Weldon, Lily St John
1920	*Puss in Boots*	Clarice Mayne, Billy Merson
1921	*Mother Goose*	Dorothy Ward, Shaun Glenville, Wee Gergie Wood
1922	*Queen of Hearts*	Mona Vivian, A W Baskcomb, Lupino Lane
1923	*Jack and the Beanstalk*	George Robey, Jay Laurier, Blanche Tomlin
Between 1924 and 1933 musicals held sway		
1924	*Brighter London*	Jack Edge, Hal Bryan
1925	*Rose Marie*	George Gregory, Virginia Perry
1926	*Sunny*	Jack Melford, Lalla Collins, Eddie Childs
1927	*The Desert Song*	Harry Welchman, Edith Day
1928	*Show Boat*	Daisy Elliston, John Coyle
1929	*The New Moon*	Jerry Verno, Eileen Moody
1930	*Stand Up and Sing*	Jack Buchanan, Anna Neagle
1931	*Bitter Sweet*	Ivy St Helier
1932	*Cavalcade*	Mary Clare
1933	*Jack and Jill*	Arthur Riscoe, Betty Davies
Pantomimes resume		
1934	*Mother Goose*	Will Fyffe, George Lacy, Kitty Reidy
1935	*Cinderella*	Jay Laurier, Helen Breen, Joan Cole
1936	*Jack and the Beanstalk*	Tommy Morgan, Dorothy Ward, GS Melvin
1937	*Puss in Boots*	Harry Gordon, Esme Marshall
1938	*Aladdin*	Harry Gordon, Renee Foster
1939	*Cinderella*	Harry Gordon, Muriel Barron, Helen Barnes
1940	*Sleeping Beauty*	Evelyn Laye, Harry Gordon
+ touring pantomime	*Cinderella*	Jack Buchanan, Adele Dixon, Fred Emney
1941	*Dick Whittington*	Will Fyffe, Harry Gordon
1942	*Jack and the Beanstalk*	Will Fyffe, Harry Gordon
1943	*Red Riding Hood*	Will Fyffe, Harry Gordon
1944	*Robinson Crusoe*	Will Fyffe, Harry Gordon
1945	*King and Queen of Hearts*	Will Fyffe, Harry Gordon
1946	*Babes in the Wood*	Will Fyffe, Harry Gordon
1947	*Humpty Dumpty*	Harry Gordon, Alec Finlay
1948	*Puss in Boots*	Harry Gordon, Alec Finlay
1949	*Dick Whittington*	Harry Gordon, Alec Finlay
1950	*Cinderella*	Harry Gordon, Alec Finlay, Robert Wilson, Duncan Macrae
1951	*Aladdin*	Harry Gordon, Alec Finlay, Robert Wilson, Duncan Macrae
1952	*Jack and the Beanstalk*	Harry Gordon, Alec Finlay, Robert Wilson, Duncan Macrae
1953	*Babes in the Wood*	Jack Anthony, Alec Finlay, Robert Wilson, Duncan Macrae

1957

1958

ALHAMBRA

STEWART CRUIKSHANK presents

Howard and Wyndhams

FIVE-PAST
EIGHT

PROGRAMME

ALHAMBRA THEATRE
GLASGOW

MESSRS HOWARD & WYNDHAM LTD.
Managing Director · Stewart Cruikshank

Five Past Eight Arrives

The new owners redecorated the theatre, installing new carpeting and cream and gold seating in the Stalls and Circle - the Balcony had to wait - and dispensing with the two aisles in the Stalls by making a central aisle. Their top manager John Stewart was put in charge.

For each new Howard & Wyndham production of a play, musical, pantomime or summer show the managing director's widowed mother would always have a box for herself on opening night, while Stewart Cruikshank always sat in the Stalls a few rows back and at the aisle, to give him room to stick out his gammy leg. After the interval he would join his mother in the box and look at the audience to see how it was reacting.

The new musical *South Pacific* arrived for four weeks, and again the next year, with its athletic chorus of sailors including a young weightlifter from Edinburgh, Sean Connery. The show's songs included Enchanted Evening, Bali Hai'i, and Younger than Springtime. One day there was extra drama when a power failure in the city resulted in storm lamps being used at the box-office. Unlike most theatres in Britain the Alhambra had a standby generator (diesel powered since 1928) which was quickly set up to light the production.

On the 6th May 1954 *Half Past Eight* said hello to the Alhambra, packing the enormous auditorium for five months. As ever *A Cocktail of Song, Laughter and Dance* headed by Stanley Baxter and Jack Radcliffe, with Molly Urquhart, Helen Norman, Kenneth Sandford, Billy Dick and many more. There was a change of programme weekly, which soon became fortnightly to let more people see the show. After opening on a Thursday or Friday, rehearsals would start the next day for the following edition. From their start in 1933 at the King's in Bath Street, produced by Julian Wylie, and followed two years later by a separate *Half Past Eight* in Edinburgh, the *Half Past Eight* revues were major successes, led often by George West, and succeeded by Dave Willis.

Italian Opera was followed by six weeks of Tom Arnold's ever popular ice-shows - this time Novello's *The Dancing Years on Ice*. The following spring was *The White Horse Inn on Ice*. Freddie Carpenter, choreographer and Howard

(above)
Evening arrivals
(opposite)
Scenes from Five Past Eight

A costume design
Programme covers

& Wyndham's director of productions, presented *Goldilocks and the Three Bears* with Jimmy Logan, Duncan Macrae, Kenneth McKellar and Principal Girl Betty Shaw. Carpenter was also producing *Aladdin* at the Royal. His first appearance in the Alhambra was twenty years before as leading dancer in the premiere of *Bow Bells*. He began as a dancer in Australia, moved to America, dancing in the Zeigfield Follies, and was brought to Britain as a star dancer by Sophie Tucker and Jack Hulbert, before becoming a choreographer and producer for stage and film.

Five Past Eight

Styling it the *Spectacular Song, Dance and Laughter* show, Stewart Cruikshank launched in 1955 the first *Five Past Eight*, running for five months each year. He always insisted that the comedians must be Scottish, the audiences expected the best, and they generated huge profits. It was a very hot almost tropical summer, and the post-war austerity transport restrictions requiring shows to start at 7.30pm ceased. *Half Past Eight* had been starting at half past seven! Now a new time of 8.05pm was chosen, allowing people to come after a day out in the sun. Hence the new name *Five Past Eight*. Saturdays became twice nightly at 6pm and 8.30pm by removing one scene in each half!

Five Past Eight was elaborately produced light entertainment, performing comedy, historical dramas, excerpts of ballet and opera, and tap routines. Dancers were very versatile, and supported up to 20 sketches, many with scene changes within scenes. Lionel Blair staged the musical numbers and the new 32 piece Geraldo Orchestra filled the pit. Hair styling was by Daniel Pediani and animals appearing were loaned by Wilsons Zoo in Oswald Street.

(above)

1954 programme cover, 1955 flyer, South Pacific flyer.

(far right)

Jimmy Logan & Duncan Macrae await Goldilocks, Michel Mills

Michael Mills, stage director and producer for this year and the next, also produced for the BBC, where he became Head of Comedy and Light Entertainment. Mills was highly inventive. He used minimal backcloths and suggestions of scenery to pack in many scenes. Big sets with more properties were for Jack Radcliffe and Jimmy Logan, followed by Olga Gwynne and singer Alastair McHarg. There was a vast number of stage hands, and four men on the flys. *Five Past Eight* shows were the ultimate with scene changes every 2 or 3 minutes, all new and put together with intensity. Alhambra earned its reputation for the fastest and smoothest changes of any theatre. So slick were the operations, and in a very advanced theatre, which often used its revolving stage, that some performers were scared of so much equipment on opening nights. Rehearsals took place in all parts of the Alhambra at the same time each morning or afternoon, including the foyer.

Sets, costumes and stage production were managed by Reg Allen, ably supported by his deputy Gordon Dickson who had been a dancer with Ballets Russe before the war, and wardrobe supervision by Madame Irene Segalla – who exercised her power over all performers! The redoubtable scenic artist **Reg Allen** became Howard & Wyndham's production manager after theatre work in Dublin. From the company's production work-shops and stores in Haymarket, Edinburgh, he was responsible over two decades for producing sets and costumes for the company's plays and musicals, five or six pantomimes across the country each year, the *Five Past Eight* shows, and summer shows in England. In addition to having very good scenic artists and costume designers he had 24 ward-robe mistresses, chief electricians, four painters, and eight carpenters. Guest designers included Peter Rice, Anthony Holland, R St John Roper and Berkeley Sutcliffe. He put each full production on and then passed it to the stage manager.

Alhambra's Jimmy Cullen contin-ued as stage manager, and his wife Greta in charge of the master light-ing control desk. Her assistant Tom MacArthur became the technical director of the Royal Opera House Covent Garden. Actress and produc-tion manager Aileen Vernon joined from the Wilson Barrett Company and became an expert stage director. Evelyn Laye made her comeback in

(below)

Five Past Eight scenes - Kenneth Sandford and Swan Ballet, Swordid Dance with Stanley Baxter and Molly Urquhart, Lionel Blair and dancers in rehearsal break.

(top)

Stewart Cruikshank, Freddie Carpenter, Dick Hurran

(centre)

Back page of programmes, Set and set models by Reg Allen

(bottom)

Reg Allen, Gordon Dickson, Madame Segalla

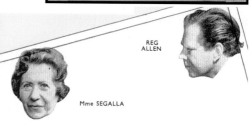

REG ALLEN

Mme SEGALLA

the musical comedy *Wedding in Paris* with newspapers reporting that "her verve and elegance have swept it to success." In pantomime *Cinderella* and her audience watched the arrival of the glittering coach drawn by four ponies thanks to Rudy Vining's Pure White Ponies. Joy Turpin, actress with the longest legs, was Prince Charming, Reg Varney was Buttons and tenor Kenneth McKellar the Lord Chamberlain. The Glasgow Herald drooled over:

(below left)
The Ugly Sisters - Stanley Baxter & Alec Finlay as Miss Carrot and Miss Beetroot, and a supermarket sketch.

> The decorations, both animate and inanimate - with the stage gracefully revolving it is difficult to distinguish between them – are often quite ravishing.
>
> Dancing, with pure ballet by Domini Callaghan and Michel de Lutry – of which Sadler's Wells would not need to be ashamed.
>
> The Ugly Sisters blended – Stanley Baxter, long and thin, Alec Finlay, short and shauchly, going to new lengths in delightful nonsense. They arrive got up as baggages in a flying cup and saucer. They picnic as root vegetables, perform a spirited ballet with a balloon, undergo fearful torment in a keep-fit clinic, and have a hard time in a haunted bedroom.

Among the new arrivals was a comedy play, led by Australia's Bill Kerr, *The Teahouse of the August Moon,* set in Okinawa which has fallen heir to all the benefits of American occupation. Jack Radcliffe and Jimmy Logan heralded 1956's *Five Past Eight* supported by Helen Norman, as ever, and joined by Joanna Rigby. Towards the end of its five months it had an Olympic Gala Show to help meet the £125,000 Scottish Appeal target set by Sir Hugh Fraser and Sir Alexander King towards sending Britain's athletes to Melbourne.

Tom Arnold's cast of 60 skaters showcased Ivor Novello's *Glamorous Nights on Ice* and in a following year Novello's musical classic had 80 skaters in *The*

(above right)
Evelyn Laye in *Wedding in Paris,* Cinderella flyer, Bill Kerr, Helen Norman & Jack Radcliffe

Dancing Years on Ice. Even today some skaters recall the effort of perpetually walking in skates to the top floor dressing rooms up and down the backstage stairs. The passenger lift was too small for so many.

Babes in the Wood

Rikki Fulton joined Jimmy Logan, Kenneth McKellar, Joan Mann, the Lionel Blair Dancers and others including Margaret Morris and her Celtic Ballet in *Babes in the Wood* in 1956/57. "Lavish, handsome and efficient as usual" wrote the Glasgow Herald:

This time Robin Hood is replaced by large pieces of Peter Pan and in no time at all we are flying like anything and on this occasion not to the Never Never Land but to the Caribbean. But the lost Boys are not in the woods there, instead Jimmy Logan and Rikki Fulton are in a variety of disguises and situations from a slapstick dinner party to a journey to Mars, and a fine lunatic concert in a barn with Jimmy playing the bull-fiddle and Rikki exquisitely refined and glassy of eye, vamping it on the piano – which is the funniest thing of the evening. Kenneth McKellar is a kind of Highland highwayman , who is enabled to sing the Skye Boat Song between hold-ups staged by a nice pair of Kind and Cruel Robbers.

Alhambra shows and pantomimes drew quality scriptwriters such as David Croft, Kenneth Little - who wrote a cascade of sketches and musical numbers, under titles like Hell Caledonia, The Glesca Waltz, Pinto's Scaretaker, My Fare Lady and The Cheery Orchard - former newspaperman John Law, journalist Alex Mitchell, Sam Cree and Stan Mars - while also being a comic performer and the genius behind Francie & Josie. In his Mount Florida house Stan Mars wrote in a special room reserved as a gag factory. He said "Josie had a rough exterior but a soft heart. Francie and Josie would be neds with a touch of the Boy Scouts about them."

Dazzling debuts

(above)
Flyers, 1956

One dazzling show presented by Jack Hylton was *Kismet* and its Arabian Nights, a new version from America's Zeigfield Theatre with sumptuous sets and costumes. Six weeks of music, movement and glitter followed the changes of fortune of a poor poet. Tudor Evans as a singer and comedian, John Cabot as Omar, and Pamela Gale, were surrounded by singers, beggars, dervishes, guards, harem women and slaves. New songs included And This is my Beloved, Strangers in Paradise, and Baubles, Bangles and Beads.

Another dazzling debut, and never shy, was Dick Hurran taking up his new role as producer of *Five Past Eight*. He had been a dancer with *Half Past Eight* before the war, moving on to be a nightclub and theatre producer and songwriter. He liked large-scale spectacle and soon created novel, highly engineered and advanced sets each year, which were not to be equalled in Britain. The shows became even more lavish. Editions changed from being fortnightly to three-weekly - such was their popularity. Hurran also enjoyed circuses and usually worked a circus into each revue. He concentrated upon the Alhambra but also kept an eye on Edinburgh's *Five Past Eight*. Dick Hurran's first *Five Past Eight* starred Stanley Baxter, Jimmy Logan, David Hughes, and Fay Lenore, with the George Mitchell Singers and Roy Kinnear. While across in Edinburgh, Alec Finlay, Rikki Fulton and Kenneth McKellar took the lead in its *Five Past Eight*.

Most years Alicia Markova and Anton Dolin's London Festival Ballet

(right)
Festival Ballet Flyer (1958), Petrouchka, Graduation Ball, David Hughes, Joan Mann, Kenneth McKellar (1956)

Immediately following Sensational Christmas Season at the Royal Festival Hall, London and Prior to Paris Festival

For ONE Week ONLY, Commencing Monday, 24th March, 1958

LONDON'S FESTIVAL BALLET

ALHAMBRA THEATRE GLASGOW

Proprietors : Howard & Wyndham Ltd.
Telephone : Central 5346

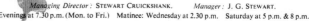

Managing Director : STEWART CRUICKSHANK.   *Manager :* J. G. STEWART.
Evenings at 7.30 p.m. (Mon. to Fri.)   Matinee: Wednesday at 2.30 p.m.   Saturday at 5 p.m. & 8 p.m.

(above)

Five Past Eight dancer costumes, Waterloo costumes (red and white satin),
Mother Goose (Columbine, Policeman, Candlestick Maker, Butcher, Pantaloon).

presented up to 14 ballets in their fortnight's visits. 1957's cast included a young Peter Darrell who would be asked to form The Scottish Theatre Ballet company in ten years time.

  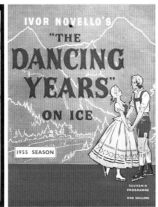 

Pantomimes continued to be the prime preserve of Freddie Carpenter, and *Mother Goose* opened with an elegant waddle. Stanley Baxter as Mother Goose and Duncan Macrae as McDrookit came together for the first time since they were in the Citizen's company, joining Fay Lenore as Principal Boy. There were also the Ross Taylor Dancers and the George Mitchell Singers, and as the Glasgow Herald commented:

(above)

Flyers and Posters

> For a breathless five minutes or so there are the Flying de Pauls (from
> Australia) - a quintet of Amazonian young women composed evidently of
> gutta-percha. It might be said that they bring the house down, except that
> with one muscular arm or leg they would certainly have propped it up again."

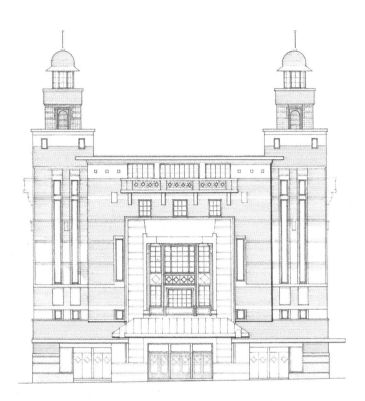

The Royal Scottish Variety Performance

1958 was an extra-special year. The first-ever Royal Scottish Variety Performance took place, attended by the Queen and the Duke of Edinburgh, almost fifty years after Sir Alfred Butt staged the first British Royal Variety performance in London.

The Alhambra was repainted every two years whether or not a Royal visit, when many other theatres were painted once in 10 or 20 years. It was staffed by between 75 and 90 people the difference being the number of casual stage hands, usually 10 rising to 25 depending on the show. Over the previous decades some smaller rooms were combined but the normal number of 18 (large) dressing rooms all with showers remained unchallenged in Britain. The huge dressing room for the chorus could accommodate 30 chorus girls. Near the stage door were the rooms of the Stage Manager, Chief Electrician, and Housekeeper (who also acted as head dresser) while under the stage was the Musical Director's office, and band room. Also downstairs was a shower room for staff, a rare feature elsewhere.

More amenity was planned beginning in 1958 when a Board Room was added below stage level. This was beautifully carpeted and furnished with gold brocade chairs, mirrors, and a fully stocked bar with crystal glasses. All very exclusive. Mrs Burnet the head house-keeper guarded it with her life!

Immaculately Clean

At the end of a day the ushers would cover all seats with white sheets. Every morning the theatre was cleaned and vacuumed, using the Clyde-Turbo system. The sheets were always restored to position. At 12 noon the Head Cleaner knocked on the Housekeeper's door to report cleaning had finished, whereupon Mrs Burnett put on her white gloves and in-spected a different area each day. Before each performance the Head Usher reported to the Housekeeper once the ushers were all in position after readying the house and removing the white sheets. He then blew his whistle to open the doors for business.

Programmes now announced "Opera Glasses have been installed for Patrons' convenience and are attached to the back of seats in the Stalls and

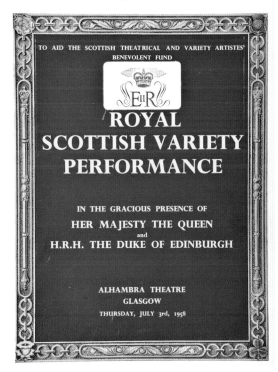

TO AID THE SCOTTISH THEATRICAL AND VARIETY ARTISTES' BENEVOLENT FUND

ER

ROYAL SCOTTISH VARIETY PERFORMANCE

IN THE GRACIOUS PRESENCE OF
HER MAJESTY THE QUEEN
and
H.R.H. THE DUKE OF EDINBURGH

ALHAMBRA THEATRE
GLASGOW
THURSDAY, JULY 3rd, 1958

(above)
Souvenir Programme

(opposite)
Royal Finale, 1958

105

Circle. Please replace after use." These could be picked up once a coin was inserted in the holder. The glasses had a gilded stamp impression - *Property of Alhambra Theatre*. Once finished being used and replaced in the holder the coin was returned.

A Silver Jubilee

Prominent amongst plays was a new comedy *The Brass Butterfly* with Alastair Sim as the Emperor, and George Cole the inventor in the Chinese court; and the premiere of *Hook, Line and Sinker*, a comedy of delinquents galore, with Robert Morley, Bernard Cribbens and Joan Plowright – the charmingly infuriating gold-digger. It was adapted by Robert Morley "who sails through the evening getting laughs with his wonderfully smooth lines and with every movement of his eyebrows." And *Duel of Angels* with Vivien Leigh, Claire Bloom and Derek Nimmo.

The *Scout Gang Show* celebrated its Silver Jubilee right where it started. *Gang Shows* filled the house, tickets for a week being sold out in one day to the public and family and friends of the 18,000 Scouts in Glasgow. The show's immaculate opening chorus in scarlet and white had the

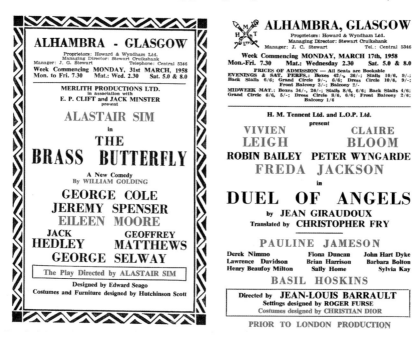

(above)
Flyers, 1958

spotlight shining on fathers and sons appearing together, with Louis Freeman conducting the orchestra – and wearing his khaki Scout shirt. In the words of the Glasgow Herald the show proved that:

> A Scout's musical talent is not confined to singing round a camp fire; the Scouts of Glasgow, whether appearing as ancient Greeks, Girl Guides (in fashionable chemise dresses) or American sailors, show considerable aplomb as revue stars.

> Audience appreciation is explained, not by the number of parents, aunts and uncles, Scouts, Guides, Cubs and Brownies in the theatre, but by the wit, pace and imagination of the show,

composed as all *Gang Shows* have been, by Ralph Reader.

While it is very properly a team affair, special mention should be made of a small boy with a small guitar who gives a hot rendering of a song "Lady Macbeth is Coming to Town."

Effects in *Gang Shows* included horses, and motor bikes and "real rain" - the rain coming from pipes added above the stage with holes put in them. To make sure the audience realised it was real, one row of pipes was aimed at the audience over the heads of the orchestra. The backstage staff at the Gang theatres were always delighted when the shows took place as volunteering Scouts were able to run the show with a minimum of input from them. Some later became qualified Technical Stage staff and managers, such as Billy Differ, others became entertainers, most notably Stanley Baxter.

Amateur companies made their mark, most frequently the Glasgow Grand Opera Society from 1958 with *Masaniello,* and *Samson & Delilah,* produced by Jack Notman. Sets were designed by Jefferson Barnes, director of Glasgow School of Art. Each year *Stars for Spastics*, often involving Scottish Television, was staged for a week with all performers providing their services without fee – finishing with a champagne reception and meal at the end of the week at the Ca'doro hosted by Reo Stakis. This year the week's proceeds helped build a new centre for the handicapped in the Paisley area.

The Royal Scottish Variety Performance

For *Five Past Eight*, producer Dick Hurran installed three powerful stage lifts which could lift the whole front, middle, and back of the main stage in differing sequences. (The two existing scenic lifts continued.)

One scene this year captivated above all – the Riviera scene with a 20,000 gallon 18-feet wide swimming pool being raised up complete with an aqua ballet and dancers, made even more visible by a giant mirror descending from the fly tower and then tilted. This was also in the special evening of 3 July 1958.

Ticket prices as high as £50 for the front stalls (equal to £600 in today's money), normally 8/6d, and a £1 for the balcony, normally 1/6d, went with other revenue from the Royal evening to support the Scottish Theatrical & Variety Artistes Benevolent Fund, whose President was theatre and cinema impresario Alex Frutin. Many Scots entertainers graced the Royal Variety performances in London over the years but this was the first in Scotland,

(below right)

Joan Plowright, Claire Bloom, Vivien Leigh, Derek Nimmo.

(below left)

Alastair Sim, George Cole, Robert Morley

Entertaining on July 3rd 1958

The Andrea Dancers, Jack Anthony, Stanley Baxter, Bernard Bresslaw, Clyde Valley Stompers, Rudy Cardenas, Grace Clark and Colin Murray, Tommy Cooper, Jacqueline Delman, Lonnie Donegan, Alec Finlay, Rikki Fulton, Geraldo and his Orchestra, Los Gatos, Margo Henderson, David Hughes, Landellans Jivers, Alan King, Fay Lenore, Jimmy Logan, May Short (Logan), Sally Logan, Alicia Markova, Larry Marshall, Alistair McHarg, Kenneth McKellar, Jack Milroy, George Mitchell Singers, Tommy Morgan, Jack Radcliffe, Janette Scott, Jimmy Shand and his Band & Dancers, Charlie Sim, Andy Stewart, Ross Taylor Dancers, Marjorie Thompson, Frankie Vaughan, Johnny Victory, Aly Wilson, Robert Wilson, Band of the Scots Guards, City of Glasgow Police Pipe Band; and a walk onstage of others in showbusiness. An edited version of the show was broadcast on radio a few days later.

(opposite)
Fay Lenore and Riviera Scene, Gang Show 1960, Queen Elizabeth enters the foyer; accompanies Alex Frutin; takes her leave of Stewart Cruikshank.

to the credit of Howard & Wyndham and members of the profession.

Security was tight and applications by letter ballot were vetted by the police, who for the evening had 70 plain clothes officers inside. But no charge to them! John Mulvaney tried to get into the building with a parcel of clean laundry ready for the next day's *Five Past Eight* but was refused and had to put it in the Central Station left luggage, before returning to the theatre. The *Five Past Eight* cast were joined by guests from both sides of the border and from America. The list was long, some 200 singers, comedians, dancers, musicians and acrobats, aided by a stage crew of 50. Sir Alfred Butt would have approved. One newspaper wrote:

(right)
Ian Menzies and Margo Henderson, The Clyde Valley Stompers, After Show Party

> Star names followed in quick succession and – surprise, surprise – there were a few adoring squeals from some of the beautifully gowned mesdames in the audience as Frankie Vaughan sizzled his way through a series of songs, but the man who stole the first half was undoubtedly American comedian Alan King. He wandered on without announcement, had us roaring with laughter in seconds, and wandered off. So casual, so smooth, so brilliant.

There was a special ovation for veteran Tommy Morgan who appeared in a running gag as a *Five Past Eight* customer who had come to the show on the wrong night. Impressionist Margo Henderson tickled the ribs and the piano keys, and

Alicia Markova performed the Dying Swan. Film actress Janette Scott partnered Jimmy Logan on stage; Alec Finlay had the audience singing with him in a medley of Harry Lauder songs; while Lonnie Donegan complete with banjo came on the Riviera scene and like all in that scene was pushed into the swimming pool.

(below)
Rikki Fulton, Janette Scott, Jimmy Shand, Jacqueline Delmar, Poster 1958, Stanley Baxter & Rikki Fulton

Frankie Vaughan enjoyed his special affinity with Glasgow, appreciating it was here he found the hit number, Give Me the Moonlight, when looking in a second hand shop. Hughie Green made a surprise appearance. Tenor Robert Wilson opened the second half and at the finale, almost at midnight, after the City of Glasgow Pipe Band joined with the Scots Guards, the whole company assembled. Kenneth McKellar in the centre front, flanked by ballerina Alicia Markova and soprano Jacqueline Delman, sang God Save the Queen, unaccompanied - after which the audience broke into Will Ye No Come Back Again?

Before the show, manager John Stewart arranged for the Boy Scouts to be on the roof at the flagpole to look out for the Royal car coming from Central Station and then to unfurl the Royal Standard, which they did. In all the excitement at the end, long taxi queues, and stage parties - thanks to Reo Stakis - the Scouts were totally forgotten. But the Scouts had gone home themselves, taking the Royal Standard as a souvenir.

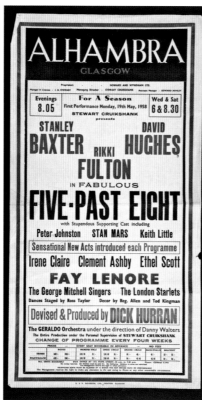

Five Past Eight

Stanley Baxter and Rikki Fulton teamed up for the first time, joined by singer David Hughes and leading lady Fay Lenore. The George Mitchell Singers, famed through television thanks to their Falkirk founder, complemented the Ross Taylor Dancers. The swimming pool also had portholes in its side through which lights shone illuminating the whole thing. Six swarthy flamenco dancing Spaniards, Las Trianas from The Lido, Paris, added to the holiday themes, as did sumptuous sets, and

A Moving Experience

An example, one year, of using the many lifts was in a George Gershwin scene for Rikki Fulton, maestro at the piano. Producer Dick Hurran set the stage all in blue. He even decreed that the concert grand pianos - hired from Patersons of Buchanan Street - be painted over with blue emulsion. Patersons found out later! The orchestra, busy playing the overture, started high up on lift number 3 at the back of the stage, which slowly descended to stage level, proceeding forward over number 1&2 lifts which were both at basement level (loaded with pianos and performers) and then placed on the orchestra lift at the pit.

As soon as the bandwagon, still playing, started to sink into the pit the other stage lifts quietly moved. Number 3 came up to six-foot above the stage to meet the Tiller Girls who flew down from the flies on a metal bridge; the second came up to half that height, complete with three pianos and three Tiller Girls; and the lift near the front rose from the basement to the stage with a Tiller Girl on each side of a smiling Rikki Fulton settled at his piano. As he began playing Rhapsody in Blue the piano's electric truck moved it further down stage in full spotlight.

trains and planes; while an enormous rain curtain was installed for Singin' in the Rain, immortalised by Gene Kelly. There was a change of programme every fourth Monday.

In 24 weeks it was seen by 328,000 people, higher than last year's 317,000, and the previous 280,000. The Edinburgh *Five Past Eight* played to 170,000 and on its closing it moved for a week to Dundee as an experiment. *Five Past Eight* would continue for the next decade, with substantial changes each year. Over 400,000 came to it at the Alhambra next year. Pantomime held sway in the winter months and the few months not already spoken for attracted musicals, followed by opera, and later by ballet.

(above)

Programmes. Effervesence of Fay Lenore, Rikki Fulton, Reg Varney and Clem Ashby. Manager's wife Mrs Stewart on the orchestra bandwagon.

HOWARD & WYNDHAM'S
Sinbad the Sailor

STEWART CRUIKSHANK
presents
Fabulous
"Five-past-Eight"
OF 1960

ALHAMBRA THEATRE GLASGOW

STEWART CRUIKSHANK PRESEN

Fabulous
**'FIVE
PAST
EIGHT**
OF 1961

ALHAMBRA THEATRE · GLAS

Fabulous Fun, Music and Dance

Later in the Royal Year, *Sinbad the Sailor* displayed the usual effects of Freddie Carpenter with well drilled dancers, much colour and elaborate scenery, including Rikki Fulton in a glorious role as a repulsively funny nurse. The Scotsman wrote:

> The Arabian Nights leap to life with alligators swimming in real pools, a giant bird which carries the hero into the frantic flies, and galleons which plunge through a cloud-chasing night.

And the Glasgow Herald signalled:

> Sinbad the dashing hero is David Hughes, melodious baritone, bearded and turbanned and as a Principal Boy unable to be the usual female in that role.
>
> Going through a condensed version of his seven voyages and collecting not only treasures but also a wife (songstress Sheila Paton) who seems to have slipped in from a "Thousand and One Nights." With Jimmy Logan and Rikki Fulton there is funny business in a barber's shop, in a fish and chip -saloon and other places, and talking of the landlord who died after drinking varnish - "he had a lovely finish." There are ballets of birds and beasts and of creatures under the sea, and the irruption of the Hassani Troupe who whirl themselves around the stage, forming pyramids and towers.

(above)
Sinbad Scene

(opposite)
Sinbad flyer, Goody Two Shoes finale set, Opera poster 1959, Five Past Eight souvenir programmes.

Now settled in the Alhambra the Glasgow Grand Opera Society staged annual seasons with the Scottish National Orchestra in the pit, usually led by Sam Borr. 1959 saw *Carmen, Nabucco,* and *Faust*. The Orpheus Club also became annual features, this year staging *Ruddigore* "with polished vitality" and the following year *The Gondoliers*. Sandy Wilson's fresh and funny pastiche of musicals of the 1920s, *The Boy Friend*, came over two seasons - "a valentine from one post-war period to another."

Radcliffe Logan and Boswell

For the next three years Jack Radcliffe and Jimmy Logan resumed their top positions in *Five Past Eight*, joined by Eve Boswell. The trio went on to hold the record of the largest number of *Five Past Eight* shows. Singer, pianist and instrumentalist Eve Boswell was a globe-trotter and recording star with shows in Britain, her native Hungary and in South Africa where she lived mainly, returning to Scotland each year to *Five Past Eight* – even playing a duet on the bagpipes with Jimmy Logan. In private life she was Mrs Trevor McIntosh and proud of her Scottish name thanks to her father-in-law from Ayr. The stage's jewelled curtain revealed more innovations each year, not just the poodles and borzois, circus scenes, winter sports scenes, nor the vintage 1908 Rover car loaned by transport magnate John Sword. Chairman and managing director Stewart Cruikshank wrote in one programme:

> The show has come of age. Edition 1 went 5 weeks, Edition 2 played capacity for 8 weeks, and the season is not even half way. The policy is to make *Five Past Eight* bigger and better than ever. We've got the theatre, the equipment, the best public of any city – and there's no reason that Scotland should not have the very best. This year 1959 producer Dick Hurran returns with ice, hydraulic lifts, giant stairways. Spectacle and lavish colours are his trump cards – and without doubt they represent the theatre's answer to the challenge of Television.

(above)
Poster 1958, Rikki Fulton - the nurse, followed by Jack Radcliffe, Eve Boswell and Jimmy Logan.

The season's attendance reached 450,000. Tourists from America booked in New York, and others from Paris and Germany booked directly. An orchestra Band Wagon was installed, unique in Britain. It could rise with players onboard, then go down when overtures finished. It could also slide across the stage silently on rails, using low battery voltage. For a special scene or finale the platform – with players playing – could rise from the orchestra pit a distance of eight feet to the stage level; then travel – still music-making – a distance of 32 feet to the back of the stage. The final lift took the band far above the stage, with the musical director Danny Walters more than 20 feet above the stage.

The adlibbing of Jack Radcliffe and Jimmy Logan engaged the whole audience, but keeping an eye on the clock, Danny Walters was under instruction to strike up the band if comedians overran. By the weekends this proved nigh impossible. Band players included trumpeter Harry Letham, known on both sides of the Atlantic, and who later moved to Scottish Television, and arranger Bobby Pagan who started as a cinema organist and later became a stalwart of the BBC radio programme The Organist Entertains.

Of the show's editions the Daily Express explained:

> The scenery revolves and tilts and slides. Great chunks of the stage zoom mysteriously up and down, elevating the entire Geraldo Orchestra, or a regiment of gorgeous girls. Half the stage suddenly becomes a real ice rink. The side of a liner slides aside and we are in the engine room, with stokers at the glowing furnace in a ballet.

A visitor returns

One morning Jimmy Logan was putting the dancers through new routines for a new sketch. The stage working lights were on, the pianist the only occupant in the pit. No scenery. Onstage the girls were in their ordinary clothes, with no make-up, some in curlers. At the stage door a gentleman asked if he could come in. He was passing by and was curious. Eventually after a few phone calls the doorman let him in. Meanwhile the piano continued as the dancers went through their paces, but the music ground to a halt and from the stage they looked to see who was the person gradually coming down the centre aisle. None other than film star Cary Grant !

He apologised for intruding, saying he was in the city to make a new film. He wanted to see the Alhambra again, many years after he had started his career on its stage as a member of the Pender Troupe of pantomimists. Sensing the girls' embarrassment of being in a mix of clothes and unkempt he invited them all, after rehearsals were finished, to join him later at his suite in the Central Hotel for afternoon tea. Wearing their best frocks and suitably coiffured the girls were delighted to go.

Evelyn Laye and Stanley Baxter led in the premiere of a comedy *The Amorous Prawn* which followed right on the heels of *Five Past Eight*. Well staged as it was nothing could stand comparison with the previous show. The

(below)
Poster 1959,
Programme 1960

Five Past Eight - *(top)* Eve Boswell; Sheila Paton and the Bluebells
(centre) The McAuleys - Jack Radcliffe, Jimmy Logan, Helen Norman; Jimmy Logan and Rikki Fulton; Jack Radcliffe
(bottom) Jimmy Logan as the District Nurse, and as the Coalman

Five Past Eight - *(top)* Bridge of Glamour, Summer Afternoon Picnic
(centre) Madame Butterfly, Transport through the Ages
(bottom) The Bluebell Girls

editor of America's Variety magazine classed *Five Past Eight* as one of the top ten shows in the world. Bids for it came regularly from South Africa and Australia, and ITV companies wanted to televise it.

In winter Alec Finlay appeared in his 15th pantomime at the Alhambra, "the opulent and funny" *Goody Two Shoes* - with Jack Tripp, Sheila O'Neill, and Ann Howard. The stylish scenery was designed by Peter Rice, noted also for his opera work.

(below)

Behind the Scenes - Eve Boswell, Jack Radcliffe, Una Maclean and Jimmy Logan, Sheila Paton

The Merry Widow

Franz Lehar's *The Merry Widow* produced by Freddie Carpenter ran for weeks in 1960, starring Vanessa Lee, Peter Graves (her husband), and Douglas Byng.

Its sublime costumes were designed by Anthony Holland who soon would help create the most imaginative designs seen in any pantomime. More of the amateur societies added to the Alhambra lists – including The Pantheon Club performing *Carousel*, in succession to *No, No, Nannette* the previous year, and joined in later years by the Lyric Club and the Theatre Guild. All their singers were keen to pass the test – were their voices able to reach the back of the theatre?

(below)

Pantomime Flyer

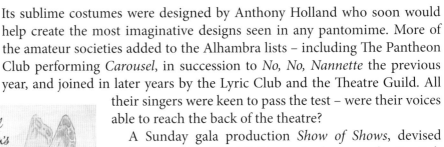

Howard & Wyndham's

GOODY TWO-SHOES

A Sunday gala production *Show of Shows*, devised and directed by Rikki Fulton, raised money for Equity's new Scottish Fund. This included three pianists perfectly playing Rhapsody in Blue on three concert grand pianos – Jimmy Logan, Rikki Fulton and Alistair McHarg who was a trained classical pianist as well as a singer. Equity Scotland's founding chairman, Duncan Macrae, wrote in the programme:

Tonight's show is to be taken as a graceful gesture. Nobody on this side, of course, is being paid. We do it tonight for the love of our mistress The Theatre, that fickle jade whose variety age cannot wither, nor custom stale.

The Bluebell Girls Arrive in Britain

To a national fanfare of publicity the statuesque and glamorous Bluebells Girls flew in from their Lido theatre headquarters in Paris, making their debut in Britain at the Alhambra. For 12 years they were the main attraction in Le Lido and now a main attraction in *Five Past Eight* for two years. Jack Radcliffe, Jimmy Logan and Eve Boswell had in their cast singer Sheila Paton, the acrobatic Carsony Brothers and, making her own wee debut, actress Una McLean from the Citizens' theatre. Her talent for comedy and timing had been spotted.

Margaret Kelly, the Bluebells founder, accompanied her troupe and appointed as Bluebell captain Audrey Mortimer now based in Paris and originally from Fife. Kelly first trod the boards as a youngster in Liverpool before joining a Scottish dance troupe Hot Jocks, touring music halls. She joined the famed Jackson Girls here and danced with them in Berlin in the 1920s before moving to Paris where in 1932, age 22, she started her own group called the Bluebell Girls.

(above)

Goody Two Shoes production conference (Freddie Carpenter talking to Alec Finlay)

There were Parisian scenes, a Roman Orgy of near Hollywood dimensions, a Viennese Ballroom reflected at a vertiginous angle in a very large mirror, and fireworks. This year Dick Hurran built a 24 foot glass tank at the back of the stage for a firework display each evening – the sparks and smoke being drawn up a funnel to a water tank at the top of the building. Major scenes included a giant Ferris wheel containing 1400 lights, and illuminated helter skelters. The stage got an electric powered moving staircase placed on an arc at the rear of the stage, allowing grand entrances from the first-floor level behind the stage.

The Bluebell Girls made their entrance on smooth stepped platforms moving in from both wings, dancing out on to a semi-circular stage in front of the orchestra. In the next edition they floated in from the side galleries on hobby horses, motors making them rise up and down to the music. The tall Bluebell Girls got all the attention, on and off stage and even when enjoying the sunshine on the Alhambra's flat roof.

To balance things up after one of their dance routines Una McLean came on dressed as a Dandelion – because she wasn't a Bluebell. Once at rehearsal Una was in the wings in tears. The staff called for Jimmy Logan who asked what the matter was. When rehearsing her lines with Jack Radcliffe she said Jack was ignoring her and directing his voice outwards. Jimmy consoled her, saying "you're not in legitimate theatre now where performers talk to each other – in variety you are always addressing the audience."

Normally Edinburgh's *Five Past Eight* went on to Her Majesty's Theatre,

(previous pages)

The Merry Widow scenes and costume designs

The Bluebell Girls Arrive

Aberdeen in August but this year switched to the King's in Glasgow before going north. (Otherwise the King's would shut for lack of summer attractions.) Directed by Michael Mills this *Five Past Eight* was led by Rikki Fulton and Margo Henderson, and for the King's it sported the new title of *Half Past Seven*. Rikki Fulton recalls that audience numbers varied, because it was not in the Alhambra. *Five Past Eight's* formula was copied in some of Howard & Wyndham's English theatres under different titles – including at Birmingham,

(above)

Music of Vienna, Roman Holiday, Eve Boswell piano set, Eve Boswell and Jimmy Logan

Liverpool, Manchester and at Victoria Palace, London (built for Sir Alfred Butt). The original title was always reserved to Scotland.

In the few weeks before the pantomime starting the D'Oyly Carte Opera company, with Kenneth Sandford and others, staged a season of Gilbert & Sullivan, opening their first night as usual with *The Mikado*.

The Entire Theatre Company

Orchestra

Stage Crew

Box Office Staff, Ushers, Cleaners, Housekeepers, Bar Staff, and Manager John Stewart *(center)*

Production Staff

Ross Taylor Dancers

Front row includes John Mulvaney, Sheila O'Neill, Jack Radcliffe, Dick Hurran, Jimmy Logan, Eve Boswell, Don Peters, Sheila Paton, Billy Dick

(right)
Highland Games
(below)
Kelpie Glade, Lizzie White Heather, Aggie fights the
Dragon, Finale

A Wish for Jamie

Stewart Cruikshank encouraged producer Freddie Carpenter, its author John Law and choreographer Peter Darrell in a new venture opening in December 1960. *A Wish for Jamie* was written round Kenneth McKellar- as Jamie - "with the songs and dances of Scotland woven into the story of the pantomime." This was Howard & Wyndham's first Scottish story pantomime, instead of a Continental tale, and the season sold out in two weeks. *Jamie* would run for years. This was the Alhambra's Jubilee Year, with first night patrons receiving a miniature of whisky with their programmes.

Set in Fairy Tale Land with comic frogs and colourful characters, Jamie's wish is that he wants to marry the laird's daughter. Jamie is the easygoing member of a family trio – Rikki Fulton his sister, and Fay Lenore his brother Donald who guards Jamie's sweetheart, Principal Girl Mary Benning, against allcomers be they laird's sons or frogs. The comic partnership is Rikki Fulton as Dame Little, and Reg Varney as Percy the English farmhand. It started with Aggie Goose (Ethel Scott), the couthy wee fairy godmother, whizzing across the stage on tartan wings. She wants to give Jamie his wish but before then the Principal Girl is captured by a menacing King of the Frogs (Russell Hunter) who offers to give Jamie his wish on condition he swaps voices with the Frog. The Scotsman called it "a vibrant whirligig of fun, song and glamour," the Glasgow Herald writing:

> Jamie sings steadily on from Burns to rock' n roll and on to a climax of almost his entire repertoire with appropriate scenes shone on the screen behind. The Five Villams do the most unlikely things at fearful pace with themselves and with Indian clubs. And Paul and Peta Page's Puppets give us a kind of resume of all the pantomime plots that have not been used this time. Western Theatre Ballet help blend it all.

For the first time in Britain the same pantomime returned in the same year as it had closed. On 5 November 1961 *A Wish for Jamie* started again only 9 months after its finale. The renewals and development of Jamie stretched far into the future. The BBC's UK Head of Light Entertainment was so impressed with it and the audience that he insisted on televising The Rikki Fulton Show in the Alhambra in front of a live audience.

(above)

Reg Varney, Rikki Fulton, Kenneth McKellar

Aggie, played by Ethel Scott

(above)

Costumes for Miss
Bluebell, Aggie, My
Love is Like a Red
Red Rose

Scottish National Ballet

In the Spring a revue *On the Brighter Side* opened with Stanley Baxter, Betty Marsden, Una Stubbs, Ronnie Barker and Amanda Barrie, who became known in *Five Past Eight*. Margaret Morris staged her Celtic Ballet in a new title *Scottish National Ballet* with Folk ballet, Scottish ballads, dances and reels, including a new ballet *To Catch A Fish*, composed by Ian Whyte founder of the BBC Scottish Symphony Orchestra. The Lyric Club made their first entry with *Perchance to Dream*, and Dame Flora Robson led in plays.

Five Past Eight for Six Months

Jack Radcliffe, Jimmy Logan and Eve Boswell created even more records, as Dick Hurran returned from his visits to Las Vegas, Paris, Rome and Beirut with new ideas and guest performers. For the girls, ostrich feathers came from Paris and jewellery from Milan. Over the record six months there were two

(above)

Paul and Peta Page,
Ballet Flyer 1961

editions, rehearsals taking place in St Andrews Halls. Of the sixteen sections five were shows within shows, each with three scenes. To great effect for his shows he used perspective scenes and tilting tables - making the stage look even bigger- and scenes like huge picture frames with artistes at angles in them.

Special effects this year included a two-ton curtain from roof to floor made to swing on its axis and become a gigantic staircase; and a passenger liner in detail 60 feet long and 20 feet high. Its destination was a South Sea Island inhabited by tartan clad natives with Jimmy Logan in a grass skirt. The tropical scene finished with Tahiti the Brave! In a cabaret scene Eve Boswell played piano with Jimmy Logan before, switching to clarinet for the melody Mack the Knife. In this Jubilee year a *Five Past Eight* postal quiz competition had prizes including a Weekend in Paris including seats at the Folies Bergere, dinner at the Lido Night Club, a mink stole and a Vespa scooter.

One "serious drama" theatregoer, John Bruce, has donated his illustrated diary to Glasgow University. His annual visit to *Five Past Eight* records his enjoyment of:

> The "New York Night Out" scenes with Boswell and Logan; and "When Knights were Bold" with the Bluebell Girls, and the George Mitchell Singers, complete with a golden staircase - A glittering scene of gorgeous mediaeval costumes and a drawbridge coming down to turn in to a grand staircase. "Follow the Sun" had a dockside with a passenger liner moving off, which changes to a paradise island featuring Jimmy Currie's Tropical Cascades - a really astonishing cascade of enormous volumes of water that was quite memorable and tremendously effective. "Getting Around" went through coaches, penny farthings, a 1911 Anzani car and a scene of ingenious illusions of young men speeding on motorbikes through a moonlit cloudy landscape.

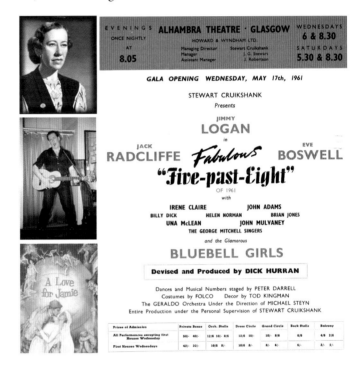

(above)

Flora Robson, Kenneth McKellar, Flyers

A Love for Jamie

Jamie returned for a third year as *A Love for Jamie*. Kenneth McKellar was now the Principal Boy and his love the Principal Girl was Jill Howard. There are scenes in Italy, with Vesuvius erupting and in Arabia. Jamie now dances, gets among wicked magicians, and stuck down the Wizard's Fatal Snake Pit, with writhing snakes, but ignored by Rikki Fulton dressed as the theatre care-taker taking visitors round the building. His real help is Aggie Goose, the fairy godmother. Joining the fun are Lenny the Lion (with help from Terry Hall), the Douglas Squires Dancers, George Mitchell Singers and Pipers of the Territorial Regiments. The Glasgow Herald hailed its return:

> Rikki Fulton bears the heat of the day as a Dame. Grotesque, agile, toothy and immensely energetic; in fearful discomfort from a very wet encounter with faulty plumbing (in a bath, shower and closet) to mal-de-mer among the

A Love for Jamie Costumes
(top) Rhinoceros Herald, Ostriche Debutante, Monkey Page
(below) Hippo Peeress, Giraffe Peeress, Elephant Peer, Cockatoo Marshal

custard pies. As a victim of physical calamity and embarrassment he spares neither himself nor the audience; and by cumulative effect – as well as such intrinsically comic turns as his schoolgirl's monologue, or the song of Lizzie, the Champion medallist of the Glasgow Highland Games – he is compellingly funny.

The pantomime came back yet again, for a fourth year, being enjoyed by 250,000 over five months each year. Endless future permutations were possible:

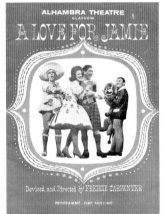

We're No Awa To Bide Awa sung by Rikki Fulton and Kenneth McKellar near the end, looks no idle promise. Jamie also sings Scots songs, Italian opera, and he and Rikki Fulton become Beatle Buds. Fulton the Eccentric Dame is really Big Lizzie McHaver, in his dead pan style of humour in every sketch.

(above)

A Love for Jamie flyer, McKellar & Fulton, Rikki Fulton and Reg Varney

Jamie moved in November 1964 to the King's to let the Alhambra extend its run of the musical *My Fair Lady*. *A Love for Jamie* also delighted at Aberdeen, Edinburgh and Newcastle with a different cast including Fay Lenore. Latterly it became *A World of Jamie,* still with Kenneth McKellar.

MUSIC HALL
TILLER GIRL

ONE DESIGN WITH
12 VARIATIONS OF COLOUR
A COMPLETE CHART OF
FOLLOWS SEES IN ENCLOSED

ST JOHN ROPER

FIVE PAST EIGHT

FRONT STALLS &
FRONT DRESS CIRCLE

FRONT STALLS &
FRONT DRESS CIRCLE

FRONT STALLS &
FRONT DRESS CIRCLE

The Starlight Room Years

Every year something new. In 1962 it was quite unique in theatre and set the pattern of future *Five Past Eight* productions – the creation of the *Starlight Room*. The Alhambra's 78 foot wide stage now cascaded into the auditorium. Britain had never seen anything like it before. It had ideas from Los Angeles, Las Vegas, Chicago and New York. This was Theatre-ama, more than equal to Cinerama.

The orchestra pit was removed and a glass apron stage with wide stairs lit from below tumbled into the stalls, being met by curved gilded stairs from new stages built in front of the boxes for singers and dancers. The stage was given a glossy non-slip black linoleum finish, polished daily and looking like glass. The band, of 12, played on a raised mushroom tower onstage. Altogether the Starlight Room had 5000 lights.

American born entertainer Dickie Henderson opened the sell-out season, with the support of singer Lena Martell (Helena Thomson from Possilpark), Una Maclean, the Tiller Girls, the George Mitchell Singers and the cabaret dancer Aleta Morrison. From America came the acrobatic dancers and instrumentalists The Charlivels, Eddie Vitch comedy mimist, and from South America the juggling Piero Brothers. The second edition from September was led by Stanley Baxter.

Welcoming the Starlight Room the Daily Express's editor wrote of Dick Hurran:

> He is Mr Spectacle of showbusiness. The man who has made the Alhambra
> Theatre, Glasgow, the home of the most lavish, glittering and glamorous
> shows in Britain. His productions cost around £150,000. They are on
> a bigger scale than anything the London Palladium can stage.

Theatregoer John Bruce's diary agreed:

> A glittering show, beautifully costumed, with a reconstructed theatre
> around the stage and the orchestra pit. The performance extends out into
> the auditorium with the side boxes now included in part of this display and
> reached by two ornamented flights of stairs. The orchestra is back staged.
> There are no changes of scene, no spectacular transformations as in last year's
> show. The entertainment was a high class variety. Lavish, in excellent taste.

Dick Hurran's new policy of using mainly London-based headliners in the coming years, such as Max Bygraves, Bob Monkhouse and Bruce Forsyth, had its ups and downs. Equilibrium was achieved by a later arrival of Rikki

(opposite)
The Tiller Girls, Fay Lenore and The George Mitchell Singers, The Starlight Room, Queen Elizabeth arrives 1963, Five Past Eight costume designs for a Music Hall scene

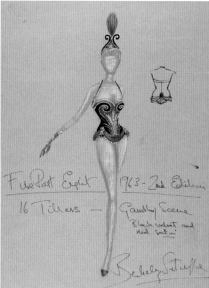

Five Past Eight 1963 - 2nd Edition
16 Tillers — Gambling Scene
Black velvet and Red satin

FIVE PAST EIGHT 1962
1920's

STEWART CRUIKSHANK
PRESENTS

DICKIE HENDERSON
AND LENA MARTELL
in

Fabulous

LENA MARTELL

DICKIE HENDERSON

FIVE-PAST EIGHT
AT THE
STARLIGHT ROOM

A GLITTERING SHOW in a
GLAMOROUS SETTING

DEVISED AND DIRECTED BY DICK HURRAN

PRODUCTION NUMBERS STAGED BY LIONEL BLAIR
DECOR BY TOD KINGMAN
COSTUMES DESIGNED BY BERKELEY SUTCLIFFE

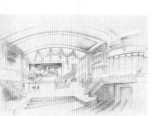

THE STARLIGHT ROOM

FIVE PAST E
Circus
8 Tillers

FIVE PAST EIGHT 1962
1920's
4 Tillers

Five Past Eight 1962, Telephone Ballet

FIVE PAST EIGHT

Fulton and Jack Milroy. At the end of each season the Starlight Room was restored to the normal theatre staging.

Royal Performance 3 July 1963

To raise money for the benevolent society a second Royal Performance took place - in essence a gala performance of *Five Past Eight*. Hurran left little time for many of Scotland's performers. The show opened with Fay Lenore, singers and dancers choreographed by Lionel Blair, and guest artistes included Eartha Kitt, Connie Francis and jazzman Acker Bilk. Bob Monkhouse did not do so well that year, and instead of a third edition *Half Past Seven* with Rikki Fulton and Jack Milroy moved in from the King's in October, before *A Love for Jamie* brought in more pantomime gold, enjoying a complete sell out – for the fourth year. Aside of his international recording career in Scots song, the works of Handel and Italian opera Kenneth McKellar judged the *Jamie* decade as his happiest performing years. Nobody could keep a straight face when Rikki Fulton appeared.

Commonwealth Arts Festival

Glasgow's celebration of the *Commonwealth Arts Festival* in 1963 saw the theatre stage performances by the Trinidad Dance Company, Royal Winnipeg Ballet, Australian Ballet and the Nigerian Folk Opera. The festival culminated in a fireworks display over Kelvingrove. More National Dance Companies started touring, notably those of Sierra Leone - rapidly becoming ambassadors for their newly independent country – Guinea, Roumania and The Philippines.

Musical societies included the Glasgow Grand Opera Society, the Orpheus Club, the Theatre Guild – presenting the first amateur performance in Glasgow of *Kiss Me Kate* - and productions by the Lyric Club, Pantheon Club and Minerva Club. The *London Festival Ballet* highlighted the artistry of their principal dancers John Gilpin, David Adams and Galina Samtsova, who later became Scottish Ballet's artistic director.

Sadler's Wells Opera and the Royal Ballet

Sadler's Wells started presenting annual seasons of opera ranging from *Cosi Fan Tutte, Peter Grimes, Rigoletto,* to *The Flying Dutchman* and *Orpheus and the Underworld*, while the Royal Ballet kept up on their toes performing amongst others *La Fille Mal Gardee , The Sleeping Beauty,* and *Swan Lake.*

My Fair Lady

On leaving London on its national tour the musical *My Fair Lady* opened in the Alhambra in May 1964 – its only venue in Scotland – performing to capacity audiences for its six months booking, and for most of its extension of another three months (in place of the *Jamie* pantomime that went off to

(opposite)

The Queen, and Duke of Edinburgh, with Lord Provost Peter Meldrum. The Queen meets Eartha Kitt, Andy Stewart, Dickie Henderson and Connie Francis.

Five Past Eight Flyer 1962.

Five Past Eight costumes - Gambling scene, Circus scene, Scarecrow Tiller Girl, Telephone Ballet, Roaring Twenties.

(above)

My Fair Lady flyer, Jean Scott

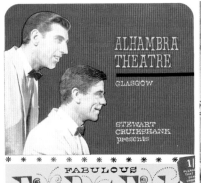

ALHAMBRA
THEATRE

GLASGOW

STEWART
CRUIKSHANK
presents

FABULOUS
Five Past Eight

PROGRAMME

Howard and Wyndham
present

'Startime'

The Alhambra Theatre
Glasgow

Playbill

the King's theatre.) Led by Charles Stapley as Professor Higgins, petite Jean Scott as Eliza Doolittle, Mercia Glossop and Zena Dare, it was seen by 650,000 people. There was an orchestra of 60, usually the Scottish National Orchestra, complete with harp, and a chorus and dancers numbering 40.

In some scenes, two revolving stages – only inches apart and moving in opposite directions - added extra excitement, and a challenge to the dancers! Songs included I Could Have Danced All Night, The Rain in Spain, and With a Little Bit of Luck. Audiences also enjoyed Cecil Beaton's striking costumes, the Embassy Ball, the stunning Ascot scene and the exhilarating coasters dance in Covent Garden.

Fol De Rols seasons opened, changing programmes weekly - led by entertainer and television compere Don Arroll, back in his home town. *Five Past Eight* took residence in the Starlight Room under the happy spell of Rikki Fulton and Jack Milroy. After five years in Edinburgh's *Five Past Eight* this was their first in Glasgow, joined by Australian pop star Patsy Ann Noble, Elaine Taylor, Clem Ashby, Ethel Scott and Glen Michael. Juggler Rob Murray was imported from Las Vegas, and ballet principals Belinda Wright and Jelko Yuresha now became regulars in Glasgow.

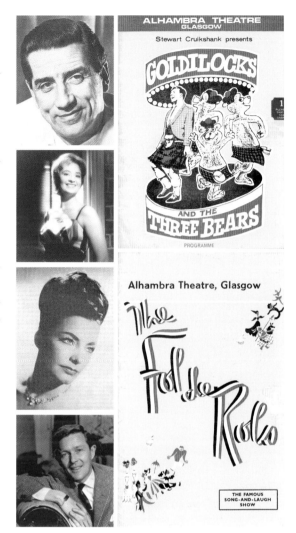

(right)
Johnny Beattie, Paula Hendrix, Lynn Kennington, Don Arrol, Fol de Rols Flyer, Goldilocks programme.

In pantomime the "Big Top Splendours" of *Goldilocks and the Three Bears* had Andy Stewart in scenes in Scotland, New York and on the Moon, while Johnny Beattie was a new Dame at the Alhambra – he was Meg in charge of the Big Top. Goldilocks was known to the grown-ups as Sheila Paton, and the Three Bears were the harmonica-playing comics The Three Monarchs.

Marlene Dietrich Captivates

For one special week the stage belonged to one woman. With musical arrangements by Burt Bacharach, this was Marlene Dietrich on another world tour. Every seat sold out. The Glasgow Herald describes the

(opposite)
Rikki Fulton and Jack Milroy - Five Past Eight programme, My Fair Lady Ascot scene, Shirley Bassey programme, Andy Stewart waits to go on stage, Marlene Dietrich, Cinderella's principals - Ronnie Corbett, Stanley Baxter and Lonnie Donegan.

Five Past Eight, and Cinderella costumes.

captivation:

> Marlene Dietrich swept on to the stage of the Alhambra last night swathed in white fur to face a receptive but uncommitted audience. Eighty minutes later flowers were being tossed on to the stage, there was the nearest thing to a standing ovation. She took us from the "Blue Angel" to Pete Seeger, and on the way she was sad and happy and funny by turn, and made us sad and happy and funny along with her.

(below)
Snow White on Ice flyer, Frankie Vaughan at Easterhouse, Frankie Vaughan Showtime flyer

> Perhaps her sad songs are the best. There is more feeling, certainly, when she sings of the follies of love and war; and that was when she reduced her listeners to complete silence, a rare feat in a Glasgow theatre. But of course there were the old favourites – "See what the boys in the backroom will have" and "Falling in love again" – sung in those swooping tones. For more than an hour, with only seconds off stage, Miss Dietrich entertained. Only Miss Dietrich at the end thought that another hour would have been too long.

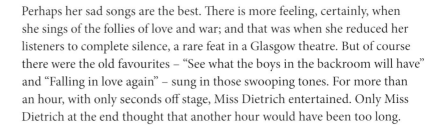

Cinderella

Tom Arnold's *Snow White & the Seven Dwarfs on Ice* with the world professional pair skating champions Carol Anne and Michael Henry whetted the appetite for another story, this time it would be the Alhambra's last pantomime and another in the charmed line of Freddie Carpenter, choreographed by Peter Darrell. In *Cinderella* the Ugly Sisters were Stanley Baxter and Ronnie Corbett, who made their entrance in a hot air balloon descending with golf clubs, and Lonnie Donegan – son of Bridgeton, jazzman and the King of Skiffle - was Buttons. Paula Hendrix as Cinderella and Lynne Kennington as Prince Charming held their own over the Ugly Sisters. The press hailed a rich evening of pantomime with transformation scenes, gaudy, gauzy, jewelled and glittering, to ravish the eye.

Frankie Vaughan and Startime

After the *Scout Gang Show* of 1967 and *Sadler's Wells Opera* the company started several seasons across two years of *Startime* fortnights – full variety with a major top-liner, starting with singer Frankie Vaughan who was also very active in his support of the Easterhouse Boys' Club which he helped promote, encouraging young lads to move away from gangs. He got his big break with Moss Empires and at the Alhambra his shows were always a great success. The staff found him a joy to work with. Howard & Wyndham gave

A Tale of Two Men

Under Stewart Cruikshank the Alhambra Theatre regularly created half of Howard & Wyndham's annual profits across its theatre division of over 20 theatres. Sadly he became terminally ill and in 1965 his deputy Peter Donald took his place as Managing Director and Chairman. By 1967 the theatre division was still making profits.

In recent years all theatrical profits continued to fall due to the effects of television, changing social habits, and producer Dick Hurran's keenness to engage television stars at high fees leaving profit margins wafer thin. But the company's investments in television companies - from their earlier association with Roy Thomson, founder of Scottish Television - brought a rich harvest in substantially greater income, rising each year. Curiously, the company sold most of its shares in television companies, for a large gain, and paid it all out to its shareholders. There was little in reserve.

Peter Donald was not of the same cut as Stewart Cruikshank, and is remembered as a humourless man, who had visions of grandeur. He wanted to open a new theatre in Hyde Park, London (a pipe dream) and to be more involved in television. Under his direction the company were joint bidders for the Yorkshire Television franchise, but did not win it.

He now diversified the company into theatre productions for others, and film and television productions, and in design graphics and equipment control systems. These soaked up money as if it was going out of fashion. All made losses. Losses from these were five times greater than the company's theatre operating division.

It is a pity that Stewart Cruikshank died.

---

him the theatre free for a week with all proceeds going to the Easterhouse project. He cajoled many stars to appear on different nights, all performing with no fee.

Top liners for Startime included Shirley Bassey - whose first appearance in the city was at the Metropole when age 16; The Shadows with Lena Martell, ventriloquist Ray Allen and Lord Charles; Harry Secombe with pianists Rawicz & Landauer; and The Seekers with comedian Norman Vaughan.

The biggest drama in 1967 was not to have a *Five Past Eight* show. Instead an ice show stuttered and plays took over. Not a pantomime but a full Festive show took its winter bow for 8 weeks - *The Frankie Vaughan Show* attracting large houses not just for the crooner but also for singer Moira Anderson, making her theatrical debut in Glasgow, joined by France's foot juggling Baranton Sisters, the tap dancing Clark Brothers of America and the Tiller Girls – including a vivid film sequence of them embarking on a BOAC plane, flying then landing, and as if by magic the girls descending from the same plane on stage.

(below)

Hello Dolly Flyer

Hello Dolly and New Investment

Hello Dolly, led by Dora Bryan brought New York joy in 1968, followed by *Startime* seasons starring Nina & Frederick with singer Edmund Hockridge and the Dallas Boys; Max Bygraves for three weeks; Cilla Black with magician David Nixon; and Frankie Vaughan with pianist Winifred Atwell. All the *Startime* shows were popular except for Bruce Forsyth, despite the attractions of the Kaye Sisters.

The company invested £150,000, most likely from the sale of the King's to Glasgow Corporation, in improving amenities even further for patrons and staff and

(above)

The Shadows Flyer, Harry Secombe, Eddie Calvert, Max Bygraves, Looking down Wellington Street, Five Past Eight Flyer 1968.

buying the property to the west of the Alhambra. The Management offices, at the Circle level, were demolished and a new Entresol Bar and reception area built for the Circle. The offices were re-sited to the top floor backstage and the existing lift renovated from basement to top. Of the new offices for the General Manager, House Manager and Assistant House Manager the first two each had ensuite facilities and showers. A new rehearsal room and more dressing rooms were planned, but were put on hold.

Five Past Eight with The Batchelors ran for three summer months, supported by Julie Rogers, Peter Goodwright, and Rawicz & Landauer who walked down stage as their pianos came from each side invisibly drawn by wires. Morecombe & Wise were rehearsing for the Festive season but due to

Attendances per house - the higher figures beiing weekend houses		
Cinderella	*1966/67 pantomime*	2000 per house
Scout Gang Show	*1967*	2000
Sadler's Wells Opera	*2 weeks*	1000-1500
Frankie Vaughan	*2 weeks*	2000 (max 2245)
Shirley Bassey	*2 weeks*	2000 (max 2245)
Sleeping Beauty on Ice	*June*	400 and then taken off
Plays in summer (replacing the ice show)		800-1200
The Shadows	*2 weeks*	1500-2200
Omsk Russian Ensemble		1000-1800
D'Oyley Carte Opera	*2 weeks*	1500-2200
Harry Secombe	*2 weeks*	1500-2000
The Seekers	*2 weeks*	1500-2200
Frankie Vaughan Show		1800-2200
1968		
Hello Dolly	*4 weeks*	1800-2200
Nina & Frederick	*2 weeks*	1000-1500 (max 2146)
Max Bygraves	*3 weeks*	1200-2000
Cilla Black	*2 weeks*	1500-2200
Play	*1 week*	300
Five Past Eight - The Batchelors	*8th June to 7th September (13 weeks)*	700-1600 (1886)
The Merry Widow (from USA)	*3 weeks*	500-1000
Frankie Vaughan	*1 week*	1000-2000 (max 2246)
Bruce Forsyth (followed by a 2 week gap until November)	*1week*	400-1000 (max 1200)
Glasgow Light Opera - Summer Song		1000-1200
Theatre Guild - Bye Bye Birdy		700-1200
Minerva Club - My Fair Lady		1700
Norman Wisdom Show	*8 weeks from 8th December*	1400-1800
1969		
Peter Pan	*First week in February*	1500-2000 (max 2246)

From the Alhambra Theatre - House Drawings Book for 1967-1969, in Glasgow University Library. Unfortunately no record book is available after Peter Pan.

illness they had to withdraw. Instead it changed to *The Norman Wisdom Show,* with Norman Wisdom and Moira Anderson. The theatre made a loss on it, the first loss for a Christmas season.

In November the company invited offers for the Alhambra, seeking £500,000 - its management claiming that there were not enough big stars nor big shows available to keep the theatre busy. (There was some truth in that because writers were concentrating on television.) Said theatre manager Herbert Lumsden "if there were we would carry on." But the company had run out of money on Peter Donald's schemes of diversification. Although offers were now being invited the manager thought the theatre would continue for about 18 months. A discount on the price was available to the city's Corporation if they stepped forward.

(below)

Nina & Frederick, Edmund Hockridge, Vince Hill, Cilla Black, Betty Grable, Ken Dodd

1969 And All That

In what would be the theatre's last year *Peter Pan* proved very popular, featuring Wendy Craig and Alistair Sim. The *London Festival Ballet* also enchanted, now including its Glasgow-born principal male dancer Ian Hamilton.

Film actress, and wartime inspiration, Betty Grable crossed the ocean on her European debut and first visit to Britain at the Alhambra. For a fortnight the house, and Waterloo Street, was crowded, not so much for the cowboy play *The Pieceful Palace* but for the legend she was. In journalist Willie Hunter's opinion Glasgow Corporation should stop thinking about preserving the Alhambra and instead should preserve Betty Grable and stop her from leaving the city's boundaries!

Howard & Wyndham announced a Farewell of the *Startime Season* but declined to say if the theatre would close. Clearly they hoped it would remain. Despite the public campaigning, and the logic of the case for it, doubts grew. All the weeks were well attended. Max Bygraves was followed by Ken Dodd with Donald Peers, Teddy Johnstone & Pearl Carr. At the end of his week Ken Dodd got a standing ovation from the full house and the audience drew tears from the entertainer as they sang Will Ye No' Come Back Again? Frankie Vaughan was joined by Winifred Atwell and impressionist Mike Yarwood; while Cilla Black in a final capacity week was supported by Vince Hill, the Dallas Boys and George Chisholm.

For months the directors forbade staff to use the word "closing" – there were to be no press statements, no guest artistes, no bouquets, no speeches – even although the Lord Provost was in the audience. However Cilla Black defied them and at the end led the audience in a medley of songs finishing with Auld Lang Syne.

Civic Deafness

From around 1960 the Corporation started demolishing whole districts of the city, decanting around 400,000 people to distant housing estates, burghs and New Towns. Apart from housing and roads it had no interest in the city's heritage. The growth of television and subsidised civic theatre continued. Howard & Wyndham started to sell their theatres, except the Alhambra, and were changing to theatre management and productions for television. Now they offered to sell their flagship to the Corporation. Despite a public campaign, and the largest petition ever, to save the theatre and use it for the city, Glasgow Corporation said NO. The Town Clerk would brook no criticism of his committees. Public engagement with the City Chambers was not encouraged. The Corporation's halls manager Tom Malarkey, now also running the King's Theatre, was very keen to take the Alhambra into the civic realm, recognising it was superior and fully up-to-date compared to its cousin in Bath Street, but the Corporation said NO.

Even the Secretary of State lent support, listing the building as a category A building of architectural and historical interest. This gave a six month reprieve, in those early days of conservation. Howard & Wyndham kept the theatre cleaned and spic and span, equipment maintained and tested, ready to open at a day's notice. But the Corporation said NO.

After the six months the company re-advertised it for sale to help pay off some of the colossal debt they built up in productions for film, television and others. It was sold for £350,000 to a property developer who demolished it in 1971 and built a monotonous dull grey concrete office block on its site. Fortunately it in turn was flattened about the year 2000 and today's new Alhambra House office building is finished in quality polished granite in a style and colour worthy of its name.

Ironically a few years earlier in 1962 fire destroyed the Corporation's famous St Andrews Halls at Charing Cross, next to the Mitchell Library. Meanwhile they arranged a "temporary" venue using an old picture house in Argyle Street for concerts and events, promising to rebuild the Halls. "Temporary" was to last almost 30 years - but if they had not closed their ears in 1969 the Alhambra would have been a superior venue.

L'Envoi

One spring evening, in 1968, Jean and I went into town wondering where we would go. Coming out of Central Station we turned left, bought tickets at the Alhambra box-office in Hope Street and went round the corner to the theatre. Clambering up the stairs to the gods we sat on the leather benches, still with their metal divisions, listening to Nina & Frederick – the silver songstress from Denmark and her husband – the Count – superbly singing their songs including Little Boxes, and Listen to the Ocean, finishing with Baby, It's Cold Outside. Throughout its career the Alhambra was equally stylish and inspiring.

Impresario Sir Cameron Macintosh wrote recently that Glasgow needs a 3,000 seat theatre so that the largest and most popular musicals in Britain could be staged and run economically. One possible candidate, he said, was the former Odeon (Paramount) cinema lying empty in Renfield Street which has a fly tower and stage. At present the journey has to be made to the far east, to Edinburgh`s Playhouse Theatre, for long-running musicals –the consolation being that the former cinema there was designed by a Glasgow architect! Another candidate would have been the Alhambra, with 60 years experience of doing it.

Pantomime Seasons Starting		
1954	*Goldilocks and the Three Bears*	Jimmy Logan, Duncan Macrae, Kenneth McKellar
1955	*Cinderella*	Stanley Baxter, Alec Finlay, Kenneth McKellar
1956	*Babes in the Wood*	Jimmy Logan, Rikki Fulton, Kenneth McKellar
1957	*Mother Goose*	Stanley Baxter, Alec Finlay, Kenneth McKellar
1958	*Sinbad*	Jimmy Logan, Rikki Fulton, David Hughes
1959	*Goody Two Shoes*	Alec Finlay, Jack Tripp
1960	*A Wish for Jamie*	Rikki Fulton, Kenneth McKellar, Ethel Scott
1961	*A Wish for Jamie*	Rikki Fulton, Kenneth McKellar, Ethel Scott
1962	*A Wish for Jamie*	Rikki Fulton, Kenneth McKellar, Ethel Scott
1963	*A Wish for Jamie*	Rikki Fulton, Kenneth McKellar, Ethel Scott
1964	*My Fair Lady*	Musical - was extended over the pantomime season
1965	*Goldilocks and the Three Bears*	Andy Stewart, Johnny Beattie, Sheila Paton
1966	*Cinderella*	Stanley Baxter, Ronnie Corbett, Lonnie Donnegan
1967	*The Frankie Vaughan Show*	
1968	*The Norman Wisdom Show*	
Summer Seasons		
1954	*Half Past Eight*	Stanley Baxter, Jack Radcliffe, Molly Urquhart, Kenneth Sandford
1955	*Five Past Eight*	Jack Radcliffe, Jimmy Logan, Olga Gwynne, Kenneth McKellar
1956	*Five Past Eight*	Jack Radcliffe, Jimmy Logan, Helen Norman, Joanna Rigby
1957	*Five Past Eight*	Stanley Baxter, Jimmy Logan, David Hughes, Fay Lenore
1958	*Five Past Eight*	Stanley Baxter, Rikki Fulton, David Hughes, Fay Lenore
1959	*Five Past Eight*	Jack Radcliffe, Jimmy Logan, Eve Boswell
1960	*Five Past Eight*	Jack Radcliffe, Jimmy Logan, Eve Boswell
1961	*Five Past Eight*	Jack Radcliffe, Jimmy Logan, Eve Boswell
1962	*Five Past Eight*	Dickie Henderson, Lena Martell; followed by Stanley Baxter
1963	*Five Past Eight*	Max Bygraves, Fay Lenore; followed by Bob Monkhouse, David Hughes, Yana; followed by *Half Past Seven* with Rikki Fulton, Jack Milroy, Joanna Rigby
1964	*My Fair Lady*	On stage for season
1965	*Five Past Eight*	Rikki Fulton, Jack Milroy, Patsy Ann Noble
1966	*Five Past Eight*	Max Bygraves; followed by Bruce Forsyth
1967	*Startime*	Fortnights throughout season
1968	*The Batchelors in Five Past Eight*	

Pantomimes and festive seasons to 1953 are listed on page 93.

Acknowledgements

Thanks are due to many for their help and interest including

the late James Hastie, Alexander McFarlane (Alhambra stage manager), William Cousins (Alhambra lighting manager), Stanley Baxter, Fay Lenore, Jean Scott McCowan, Carey Wilson, Maureen Dickson, Ian Stewart, William Glover, Raymond Stoddart, Peter Hamilton, David M Walker, John MacLellan, Joseph Jeffrey, Clemence Watt (and the archive of the late John Watt), David Weston, Graeme Cruickshank, Carol Seymour-Newton (of the Butt family), Gordon Irving, Robert Bain, William Gallacher, Colin Calder, Mike Eyre and John Hepburn.

Glasgow University Library Special Collections - Scottish Theatre Archive, Mitchell Library, Glasgow City Archives, People's Palace Glasgow, Perth & Kinross Council – Margaret Morris Movement at the Ferguson Gallery, National Archives of Scotland, Royal Commission on the Ancient & Historical Monuments of Scotland, National Library of Scotland – Scottish Screen Archive, Alexandra Palace Television Society.

Illustrations -

Many are from private collections and others are from organizations, including – Glasgow University Library Special Collections - Scottish Theatre Archive, Mitchell Library, Glasgow City Archives, People's Palace Glasgow, Perth & Kinross Council - Margaret Morris Movement at the Ferguson Gallery, National Library of Scotland - Scottish Screen Archive, Alexandra Palace Television Society, and the Royal Commission on the Ancient & Historical Monuments of Scotland who reserve the Crown Copyright on the auditorium architectural photographs shown on pages 16, 17, 21 and 26.